Managing Office 365 Identities and Requirements
Second Edition

Orin Thomas

Exam Ref 70-346 Managing Office 365 Identities and Requirements, Second Edition

Published with the authorization of Microsoft Corporation by:
Pearson Education, Inc.

Copyright © 2018 by Orin Thomas

ISBN-13: 978-1-5093-0479-0
ISBN-10: 1-5093-0479-7

Library of Congress Control Number: 2017949563

1 17

Trademarks

Microsoft and the trademarks listed at https://www.microsoft.com on the "Trademarks" webpage are trademarks of the Microsoft group of companies. All other marks are property of their respective owners.

Warning and Disclaimer

Every effort has been made to make this book as complete and as accurate as possible, but no warranty or fitness is implied. The information provided is on an "as is" basis. The authors, the publisher, and Microsoft Corporation shall have neither liability nor responsibility to any person or entity with respect to any loss or damages arising from the information contained in this book or programs accompanying it.

Special Sales

For information about buying this title in bulk quantities, or for special sales opportunities (which may include electronic versions; custom cover designs; and content particular to your business, training goals, marketing focus, or branding interests), please contact our corporate sales department at corpsales@pearsoned.com or (800) 382-3419.

For government sales inquiries, please contact governmentsales@pearsoned.com.

For questions about sales outside the U.S., please contact intlcs@pearson.com.

Editor-in-Chief	Greg Wiegand
Senior Acquisitions Editor	Laura Norman
Development Editor	Troy Mott
Managing Editor	Sandra Schroeder
Senior Project Editor	Tracey Croom
Editorial Production	Backstop Media
Copy Editor	Christina Rudloff
Indexer	Julie Grady
Proofreader	Christina Rudloff
Technical Editor	Tim Warner
Cover Designer	Twist Creative, Seattle

Contents at a glance

Contents

What do you think of this book? We want to hear from you!

Microsoft is interested in hearing your feedback so we can continually improve our books and learning resources for you. To participate in a brief online survey, please visit:

https://aka.ms/tellpress

Chapter 2 Plan and Implement Networking and Security in Office 365 29

Chapter 3   Manage cloud identities   63

**Chapter 4   Implement and manage identities by using
             Azure AD Connect   97**

**Chapter 5   Implement and manage federated identities
             single sign on   137**

**Chapter 6   Monitor and troubleshoot Office 365
              availability and usage   193**

Introduction

The 70-346 exam deals with advanced topics that require candidates to have an excellent working knowledge of both Office 365 and Windows Server. Some of the exam comprises topics that even experienced Office 365 and Windows Server administrators may rarely encounter unless they are consultants who deploy new Office 365 tenancies on a regular basis. To be successful in taking this exam, candidates not only need to understand how to deploy and manage Office 365, they need to understand how to integrate Office 365 with an on-premises Active Directory environment. They also need to keep up to date with new developments with Office 365, including new features and changes to the interface.

Candidates for this exam are Information Technology (IT) Professionals who want to validate their advanced Office 365 and Windows Server management skills, configuration skills, and knowledge. To pass this exam, candidates require a strong understanding of how to provision Office 365, plan and implement networking and security in Office 365, manage cloud identities, configure and manage identity synchronization between on-premises and cloud Active Directory instances, implement and manage federated identities as well as have the ability to monitor and troubleshoot Office 365 availability and usage. To pass, candidates require a thorough theoretical understanding as well as meaningful practical experience implementing the technologies involved.

This edition of this book covers Office 365 and the 70-346 exam objectives circa mid-2017. As Office 365 evolves, so do the Office 365 exam objectives, so you should check carefully if any changes have occurred since this edition of the book was authored and study accordingly.

This book covers every exam objective as of mid-2017, but it does not cover every exam question. Only the Microsoft exam team has access to the exam questions themselves and Microsoft regularly adds new questions to the exam, making it impossible to cover specific questions. You should consider this book a supplement to your relevant real-world experience and other study materials. If you encounter a topic in this book that you do not feel completely comfortable with, use the links you'll find in text to find more information and take the time to research and study the topic. Great information is available on TechNet, through MVA courses, and in blogs and forums.

Microsoft certifications

Microsoft certifications distinguish you by proving your command of a broad set of skills and experience with current Microsoft products and technologies. The exams and corresponding certifications are developed to validate your mastery of critical competencies as you design and develop, or implement and support, solutions with Microsoft products and technologies both on-premises and in the cloud. Certification brings a variety of benefits to the individual and to employers and organizations.

> **MORE INFO** **ALL MICROSOFT CERTIFICATIONS**
>
> For information about Microsoft certifications, including a full list of available certifications, go to *http://www.microsoft.com/learning/en/us/certification/cert-default.aspx*.

Free ebooks from Microsoft Press

From technical overviews to in-depth information on special topics, the free ebooks from Microsoft Press cover a wide range of topics. These ebooks are available in PDF, EPUB, and Mobi for Kindle formats, ready for you to download at:

https://aka.ms/mspressfree

Check back often to see what is new!

Errata, updates, & book support

We've made every effort to ensure the accuracy of this book and its companion content. You can access updates to this book—in the form of a list of submitted errata and their related corrections—at:

https://aka.ms/examref3462E/errata

If you discover an error that is not already listed, please submit it to us at the same page.

If you need additional support, email Microsoft Press Support at *mspinput@microsoft.com*.

To download a list of all URLs mentioned in this book go to: *https://aka.ms/examref3462E/downloads*

Please note that product support for Microsoft software and hardware is not offered through the previous addresses. For help with Microsoft software or hardware, go to *https://support.microsoft.com*.

We want to hear from you

At Microsoft Press, your satisfaction is our top priority, and your feedback our most valuable asset. Please tell us what you think of this book at:

https://aka.ms/tellpress

The survey is short, and we read every one of your comments and ideas. Thanks in advance for your input!

Stay in touch

Let's keep the conversation going! We're on Twitter: *http://twitter.com/MicrosoftPress*.

Important: How to use this book to study for the exam

Certification exams validate your on-the-job experience and product knowledge. To gauge your readiness to take an exam, use this Exam Ref to help you check your understanding of the skills tested by the exam. Determine the topics you know well and the areas in which you need more experience. To help you refresh your skills in specific areas, we have also provided "Need more review?" pointers, which direct you to more in-depth information outside the book.

The Exam Ref is not a substitute for hands-on experience. This book is not designed to teach you new skills.

We recommend that you round out your exam preparation by using a combination of available study materials and courses. Learn more about available classroom training at *https://www.microsoft.com/learning*. Microsoft Official Practice Tests are available for many exams at *https://aka.ms/practicetests*. You can also find free online courses and live events from Microsoft Virtual Academy at *https://www.microsoftvirtualacademy.com*.

This book is organized by the "Skills measured" list published for the exam. The "Skills measured" list for each exam is available on the Microsoft Learning website: *https://aka.ms/examlist*.

Note that this Exam Ref is based on publicly available information and the author's experience. To safeguard the integrity of the exam, authors do not have access to the exam questions.

CHAPTER 1

Provision Office 365

Setting up an Office 365 tenancy is straightforward as long as you have a good understanding of what you need to have ready before you provision the tenancy, and what steps you need to take immediately after you provision the tenancy so that you can start seamlessly moving workloads into the cloud.

Skills in this chapter

- Provision tenants
- Add and configure custom domains
- Plan a pilot

> **IMPORTANT**
>
> *Have you read page xv?*
>
> It contains valuable information regarding the skills you need to pass the exam.

Skill 1.1: Provision tenants

This skill deals with the basic process of setting up an Office 365 tenancy. To master this skill you'll need to understand some of the prerequisites, such as what you must think about before signing up for an Office 365 subscription, what an Office 365 tenant name is, what the different administrator roles are, and what to manage regarding tenant subscriptions and licensing.

> **This covers the following topics:**
> - Configure the tenant name
> - Tenant region
> - Initial global administrator
> - Administrator roles
> - Manage tenant subscriptions and licensing
> - Configure tenant for new features and updates

Configure the tenant name

When you set up your Office 365 subscription, you specify a tenant name in the form of *name*.onmicrosoft.com, where *name* is the name you want to assign to your organization's tenancy. This name has to be unique and no two organizations can share the same tenant name. The tenant name cannot be changed after you configure your Office 365 subscription.

You can assign a domain name that you own to the tenant so that you don't have to use the tenant name on a regular basis. For example, you might sign up to an Office 365 subscription with the tenant name contoso.onmicrosoft.com. Any accounts you create will use the contoso.onmicrosoft.com email suffix for their Office 365 mailboxes. Once you've set up Office 365, however, you can assign a custom domain name and have the custom domain name used as the primary email suffix. For example, assuming that you owned the domain name contoso.com, you could configure your tenancy to use the custom domain name contoso.com with the contoso.onmicrosoft.com tenancy. You'll learn more about using custom domains later in this chapter.

While you can configure a custom domain name to be the default domain name and use the custom domain name exclusively when performing Office 365 related tasks, you won't be able to remove the tenant name. The tenant name chosen at setup remains with the subscription over the course of the subscription's existence.

> **MORE INFO** ONMICROSOFT.COM DOMAIN
>
> You can learn more about initial onmicrosoft.com domains at: *https://support.office.com/en-us/article/Domains-FAQ-1272bad0-4bd4-4796-8005-67d6fb3afc5a*.

Tenant region

Tenant region determines which Office 365 services will be available to the subscription, the taxes that will be applied as a part of the subscription charges, the billing currency for the subscription, and the Microsoft datacenter that will host the resources allocated to the subscription. For example, selecting United States for a region will mean that your organization's Office 365 tenancy is allocated resources in a United States datacenter. Selecting New Zealand currently means that your organization's Office 365 will be allocated resources in a datacenter in Australia because this is currently the closest Microsoft datacenter to New Zealand.

Unlike other Office 365 settings, you cannot change the tenant region once you have selected it. The only way to alter a tenant region is to cancel your existing subscription and to create a new subscription. Selecting the correct tenant is very important from a compliance perspective and there are many stories of consultants in countries outside the US setting up US tenancies, only to find out later that they need to recreate the tenancy because customer data is stored outside the associated organization's national borders.

Administrator roles

There are five Office 365 management roles that Office 365 users can be assigned as follows:

- **Global administrator**   This role provides you with access to all administrative features. Users assigned this role are the only users able to assign other admin roles. More than one Office 365 user account can be assigned the global admin role. The first tenancy account created when you sign up for Office 365 is automatically assigned the global admin role. This role has the most rights of any available role.

- **Billing administrator**   This role gives you the ability to make purchases, manage subscriptions, manage support tickets, and monitor service health.

- **Password administrator**   This role allows you to reset the passwords of most Office 365 user accounts, except those assigned the global admin, service admin, or billing roles. Users assigned the password admin role can reset the passwords of other users assigned the password admin role.

- **Service administrator**   This role allows you to manage service requests and monitor service health.

- **User management administrator**   This role allows users to reset passwords and monitor service health. They can also manage user accounts, user groups, and service requests. Users assigned this role are unable to delete accounts assigned the global admin role; create other admin roles; or reset passwords for users assigned the billing, global, or service admin roles.

There are also roles that are associated with specific services that are enabled for the subscription. These allow management of specific Office 365 services rather than Office 365 itself. These roles include:

- Dynamics 365 service administrator
- Exchange administrator
- Skype for Business administrator
- Power BI service administrator
- SharePoint Administrator

To assign a user the global admin role, perform the following steps:

1. In the Office 365 Admin Center, select the Active Users node under the Users node as shown in Figure 1-1.

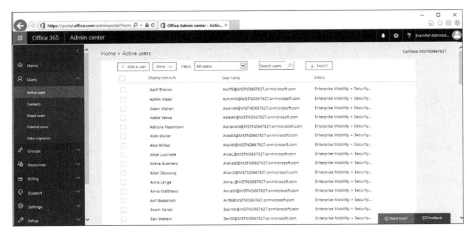

FIGURE 1-1 Active Users

2. In the Active Users node, select the user that you want to assign global admin privileges to. This will open the user's properties page, shown in Figure 1-2.

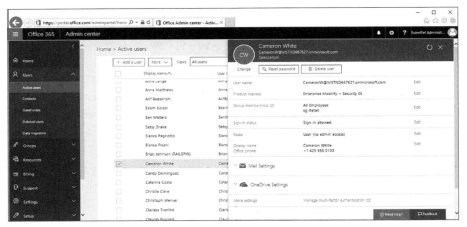

FIGURE 1-2 Select User

3. On the user properties page, click Edit next to Roles.

4. On the Edit User Roles page, select the Global Administrator role as shown in Figure 1-3 and provide an email address where password reset information can be sent. Ensure that this account is secure and protected by two-factor authentication. Click Save to apply the changes.

FIGURE 1-3 Global Administrator

MORE INFO ADMINISTRATOR ROLES

You can learn more about Office 365 Permissions at: *https://support.office.com/en-us/article/Assigning-admin-roles-eac4d046-1afd-4f1a-85fc-8219c79e1504.*

Manage tenant subscriptions and licenses

You can manage Office 365 tenant subscriptions from the Subscriptions node, which is under the Billing node and is shown in Figure 1-4.

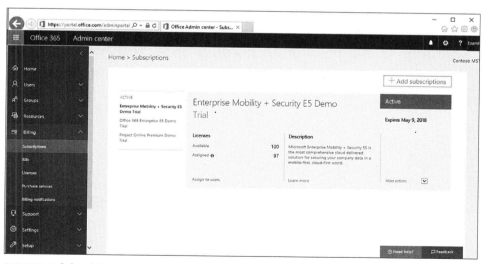

FIGURE 1-4 Subscriptions node

MORE INFO Tenant subscriptions and licenses

You can learn more about tenant subscriptions and licenses at: *https://support.of-fice.com/en-us/article/Billing-in-Office-365-for-business-%e2%80%93-Admin-Help-ea7bf1b2-1c2f-477f-a813-313e3ce0d896.*

Assigning licenses

Office 365 users require licenses to use Outlook, SharePoint Online, Skype for Business (formerly Lync Online), and other services. Users who have been assigned the global administrator or user management administrator roles can assign licenses to users when creating new Office 365 user accounts or can assign licenses to accounts that are created through directory synchronization or federation.

When a license is assigned to a user, the following occurs:

- An Exchange Online mailbox is created for the user.
- Edit permissions for the default SharePoint Online team site are assigned to the user.
- The user will have access to Skype for Business features associated with the license.
- For Office 365 ProPlus, the user will be able to download and install Microsoft Office on up to five computers running Windows or Mac OSX.

You can view the number of valid licenses and the number of those licenses that have been assigned on the Licenses node, which is underneath the Billing node in the Office 365 Admin Center. This node is shown in Figure 1-5.

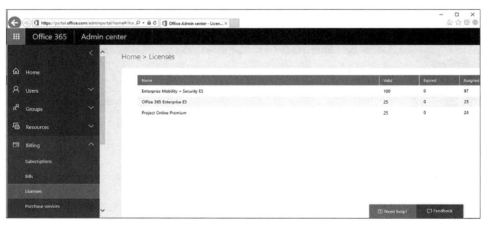

FIGURE 1-5 Licenses node

You can assign a license to a user by editing the properties of the user. To do this, select the user's account in the Office 365 Admin Center and then click Edit next to Product Licenses. On the Licenses tab of the user's properties, you can assign a license configuring the slider next to each license type. Figure 1-6 shows the Product licenses page of an Office 365 user.

FIGURE 1-6 User license

> **MORE INFO** Assigning licenses
>
> You can learn more about assigning licenses at: *https://support.office.com/en-us/article/Assign-or-unassign-licenses-for-Office-365-for-business-997596b5-4173-4627-b915-36abac6786dc.*

Resolving license conflicts

License conflicts occur when you have assigned more licenses than you have purchased. Methods that you can use to resolve this problem include:

- **Purchasing more licenses**   This resolves the issue by ensuring that the number of licenses being consumed matches the number of licenses that have been purchased.
- **Removing licenses from existing users**   You can resolve license conflicts by removing licenses from existing users so that the number of licenses being consumed matches the number of licenses that has been purchased.
- **Deleting users**   In many cases, license conflicts occur because users who are no longer associated with the organization are still consuming licenses. Deleting these users from Office 365 will release the licenses assigned to these users.

> **MORE INFO** RESOLVING LICENSE CONFLICTS
>
> You can learn more about resolving license conflicts at: *https://support.office.com/en-us/article/Resolve-license-conflicts-796f7eda-b1f8-479a-adee-bd9226ca47ec.*

Configure tenant for new features and updates

You can configure your tenancy so that some or all users get new features and updates faster than those generally available to Office 365 customers. The difference between these is as follows:

- **Standard Release** With this option, users will only be given updates as they become generally available to Office 365 customers. This option is suitable when an organization wants to minimize the amount of retraining it does of its employees to deal with new features.
- **First Release** With this option, users are given updates as they are released. This may mean that software functionality changes with an update. While suitable for users comfortable with change, many organizations avoid using First Release because they prefer a slower cadence when it comes to the introduction of new features.

You configure whether users have the Standard Release or First Release option applied by performing the following steps:

1. In the Office 365 Admin Center, select Organization Profile under Settings.
2. In the Release Preferences section, click Edit.
3. On the Release Preferences page, shown in Figure 1-7, choose the option you want to have apply to your organization and click Next. If you choose First Release For Selected Users, you can select specific users to get First Release updates while other users get Standard Release updates.

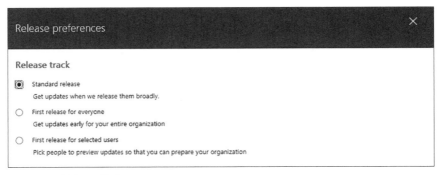

FIGURE 1-7 Release Preferences

MORE INFO **STANDARD OR FIRST RELEASE OPTIONS**

You can learn more about Standard or First Release options at: *https://support.office.com/en-us/article/Set-up-the-Standard-or-First-Release-options-in-Office-365-3b3adfa4-1777-4ff0-b606-fb8732101f47.*

Skill 1.2: Add and configure custom domains

This skill deals with configuring Office 365 to use a custom domain name, such as contoso. com, that your organization owns rather than an Office 365 tenant name, like contoso.onmicrosoft.com. To master this skill you'll need to understand the steps that you need to take to configure Office 365 to use a domain name that your organization has registered.

> **This covers the following topics:**
> - Specify domain name
> - Confirm ownership
> - Specify domain purpose
> - Move ownership of DNS to Office 365
> - Update and verify domain settings

Specify domain name

The first step in configuring Office 365 to use a custom domain name is to add the name of the custom domain name to Office 365. To add a custom domain to Office 365, perform the following steps:

1. In the Office 365 Admin Center, click Domains under Setup as shown in Figure 1-8.

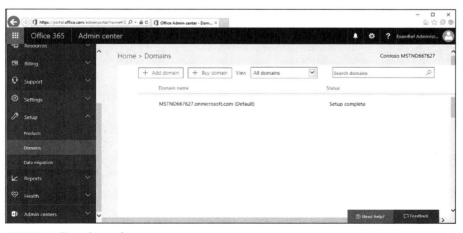

FIGURE 1-8 Domains node

2. If your organization already has a domain, click Add a domain. The alternative is to buy a domain through Office 365 and GoDaddy. The advantage of buying through GoDaddy is that you can have the entire process of assigning a custom domain to Office 365 occur automatically. If your organization's domain is already hosted elsewhere, you'll instead have to confirm ownership by configuring special TXT or MX records. You can't use the Buy Domain option with a trial account.

3. When you click Add A Domain, you are presented with the New Domain page. Enter the name of the existing domain you want to configure as shown in Figure 1-9 and click Next.

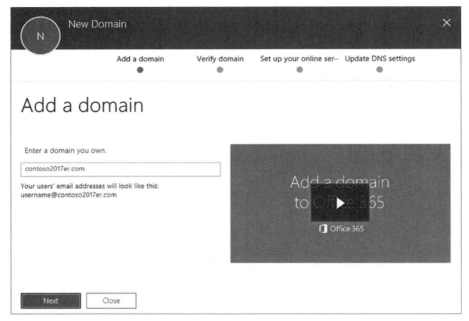

FIGURE 1-9 Add a new domain in Office 365

4. This will begin the process of adding the domain, but you'll need to confirm ownership before you can use the domain.

Confirm ownership

You can only use a custom domain name with Office 365 if your organization owns the domain name. Microsoft requires that you perform a series of DNS configuration changes to the domain name that will prove that your organization controls and has ownership of the domain.

To confirm ownership of your organization's domain, perform the following steps:

1. Once you've specified the domain you want to add, you verify the domain on the Verify domain page. This involves adding a TXT or MX record with the properties listed on the verify domain page show in Figure 1-10 to the DNS zone. You do this by configuring the DNS zone with the DNS provider.

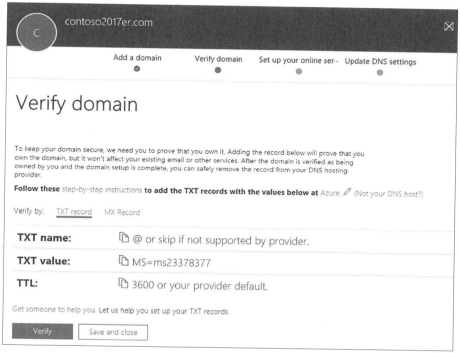

FIGURE 1-10 Verify Domain

2. Figure 1-11 shows the TXT record configured as part of the DNS zone, contoso2017er.com, hosted in DNS on Microsoft Azure.

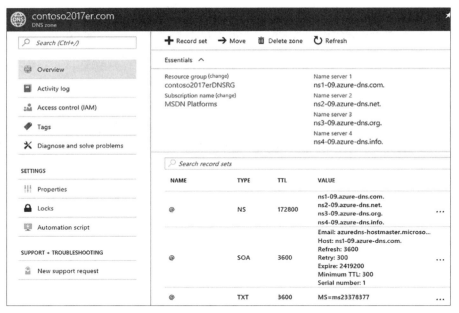

FIGURE 1-11 TXT record in Azure DNS

3. Once you have added the record, click Verify. Office 365 will then attempt to confirm the presence of the record. Depending on how DNS is configured, this may take up to 15 minutes.

> **MORE INFO VERIFYING THE DOMAIN NAME**
>
> You can learn more about verifying the domain name at: *https://support.office.com/en-in/article/Verify-your-domain-in-Office-365-6383f56d-3d09-4dcb-9b41-b5f5a5efd611.*

Specify domain purpose

By configuring a custom domain's purpose, you can choose how it will be used with Office 365. For example, you might want to use one custom domain as an email suffix, and another custom domain for use with Skype for Business. You can only configure a domain purpose once you've verified the DNS zone.

1. To configure domain purpose, either continue the wizard after verifying the DNS zone, or click on DNS management on the Domain's properties page, as shown in Figure 1-12.

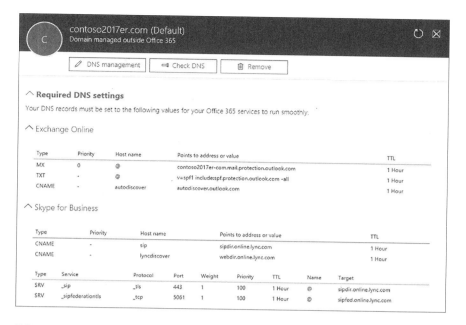

FIGURE 1-12 Domain settings

2. It's possible, when verifying a domain, to configure Office 365 to perform the rest of the DNS configuration automatically or perform this configuration manually as shown in Figure 1-13.

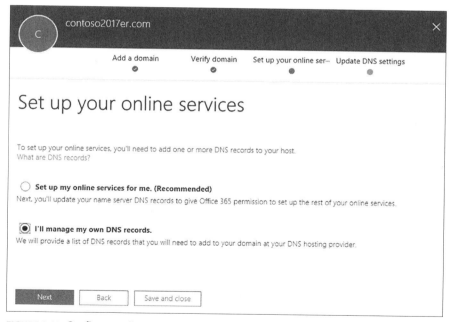

FIGURE 1-13 Configure online services

3. When you choose to perform setup manually, Office 365 will present you with a list of records that you need to add to the DNS zone as shown in Figure 1-14.

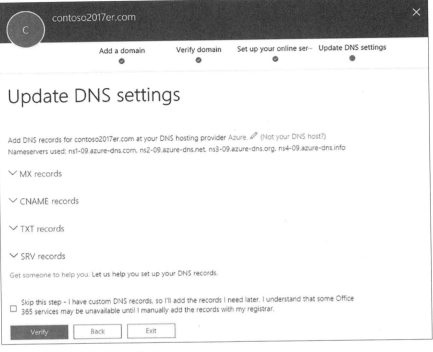

FIGURE 1-14 Update DNS settings

4. An example of the records that need to be added to the contoso2017ER.com zone to allow it to support a demo Office 365 tenancy are listed in Table 1-1. All records need to be configured with a TTL of 3600 and the MX record with a priority of 0.

TABLE 1-1: Office 365 DNS records

Type	Host name	Value
MX	@	contoso2017er-com.mail.protection.outlook.com
CNAME	Autodiscover	autodiscover.outlook.com
CNAME	Sip	sipdir.online.lync.com
CNAME	Lyncdiscover	webdir.online.lync.com
CNAME	Msoid	clientconfig.microsoftonline-p.net
CNAME	Enterpriseregistration	enterpriseregistration.windows.net
CNAME	Enterpriseenrollment	enterpriseenrollment.manage.microsoft.com
TXT	@	V=spf1 include:spf.protection.outlook.com -all

It will also be necessary to add two SRV records similar to those shown in Figure 1-15.

FIGURE 1-15 SRV records

5. Once you have added all SRV records, click Verify to ensure that the records have been configured correctly. When informed that your domain and email addresses are all set up, as shown in Figure 1-16, click Finish.

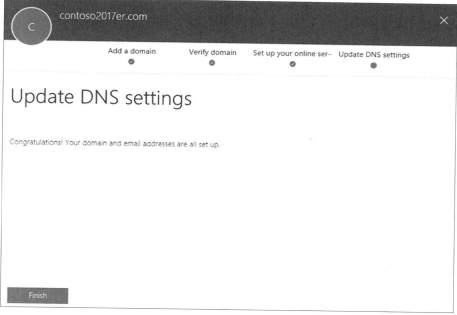

FIGURE 1-16 Complete domain configuration

Move ownership of DNS to Office 365

You can change the name servers that host your custom domain from the original registrar to Office 365. The method that you use to do this depends on the domain registrar that currently hosts the records that point to the name servers associated with the custom domain.

You can only move ownership of DNS to Office 365 if you have gone through the process of confirming that your organization owns the domain through the configuration of the appropriate TXT records.

To move the domain ownership to Office 365, you need to configure the following settings:

- **Primary name server** ns1.bdm.microsoftonline.com
- **Secondary name server** ns2.bdm.microsoftonline.com

> **MORE INFO CHANGE NAME SERVER TO OFFICE 365**
>
> You can learn more about moving to having Office 365 function a name server for a custom domain at: *https://support.office.com/en-gb/article/Change-nameservers-to-Office-365-a46bec33-2c78-4f45-a96c-b64b2a5bae22*.

Update and verify domain settings

Should you need to determine whether you have the correct DNS settings, for example when you have changed to a new DNS provider, you can use the Check DNS button on the Domain page to verify that DNS is configured correctly. This will perform a check of the DNS zone. If the settings are correct, you will be presented with a message informing you that all DNS records are correct as shown in Figure 1-17. If a setting is incorrect, the problematic setting will be listed.

FIGURE 1-17 Check DNS settings

EXAM TIP

Remember what type of DNS record you have to manually configure to confirm ownership of a custom domain.

Skill 1.3: Plan a pilot

This skill deals with planning an Office 365 pilot project. To master this skill you'll need to understand the steps involved in planning a successful Office 365 pilot project, including determining a cohort of pilot users, determining which workloads should not be migrated to Office 365, leveraging the Office 365 on-ramp tool, having a test plan, and configuring email accounts for pilot users.

This covers the following topics:

- Designate pilot users
- Identify workloads that don't require migration
- Run the Office 365 Health, Readiness, and connectivity checks
- Run IDFix
- Create a test plan or use case
- Connect existing email accounts for pilot users
- Service descriptions
- FastTrack Center

Designate pilot users

When selecting users for the Office 365 pilot, you need to ensure that you select a variety of users that represents the organization in its entirety. Part of the reason for the pilot is to identify potential pitfalls. For example, you want to figure out that there's a particular on-premises requirement for a group of workers in the accounting department before you migrate their workloads to Office 365. Figuring this out beforehand is much better than having to work out how to roll the accounting users back on-premises after the rest of the organization has migrated to Office 365.

The first step in selecting users for a pilot program is to determine how many users you want to include in the pilot program. Successful pilot programs often attempt to use a minimum of 5% of the potential group to be migrated. This 5% of pilot users should meet the following general criteria:

- **Full-time employees of the organization**   Full-time employees will be working with the new technology during normal work hours. Part-time employees may be more sporadic in their interaction with the technology and may be less able to provide useful feedback across the pilot period.

- **Representative of the organization**   Pilot users need to be from different parts of the organization. They need to have a mix of age, experience, and seniority.

- **Have been with the organization a minimum of six months**   This ensures that the pilot users are familiar with normal organizational procedures.

- **Already trained on the software that they will be using**   For example, if the pilot program involves moving to online mailboxes, pilot users should already be familiar with Outlook. If the pilot program means moving to an online version of SharePoint that the pilot users are already familiar with the on-premises deployment of SharePoint.

- **Willingness to provide feedback**   One of the most important aspects of a pilot program is hearing what works and what does not. Pilot users who don't provide both positive and negative feedback aren't providing you with the information necessary to allow you to determine if a full implementation of Office 365 for your organization will be successful.

Identify workloads that don't require migration

When planning an Office 365 pilot, an important thing to realize is that not all workloads need to be migrated to Office 365. Implementing Office 365 is not an all-or-nothing proposition. While it's possible to have all user accounts, Exchange mailboxes, Skype for Business infrastructure, and SharePoint sites hosted in Office 365, it's also possible to configure a hybrid deployment where these services are both on-premises and in the cloud. For example, you could have a deployment where only a fraction of your organization's user accounts are native to Office 365, some mailboxes are hosted on-premises, and some are hosted in Office 365 cloud. Your organization's SharePoint deployment could even be spread across servers in your local datacenter and others in Microsoft datacenters.

As part of your pilot, you should identify which workloads you don't need to migrate to Office 365. The factors that influence this decision will vary depending on your organization. Factors also vary depending on your region. Most countries don't have local Microsoft datacenters, which might mean that moving workloads to Office 365 means moving workloads across national borders. For some workload types, this may not present a problem; for other workload types, such as for workloads that deal with confidential medical data, it may not be possible to migrate the workloads across borders without contravening local legislation.

> **MORE INFO** **HYBRID DEPLOYMENTS**
>
> You can learn more about hybrid deployments at: *https://support.office.com/en-us/article/Office-365-integration-with-on-premises-environments-263faf8d-aa21-428b-aed3-2021837a4b65.*

Run the Office 365 Health, Readiness, and Connectivity checks

A variety of diagnostic tools, including tools that allow you to assess an organization's readiness to deploy Office 365, are available at *https://portal.office.com/tools*. One of these tools is the Office 365 Health, Readiness, and Connectivity Checks tool.

Running the tool involves performing the following steps:

1. Determine whether you want to perform Quick or Advanced checks. The Quick checks will perform rudimentary checks that are complete in a few minutes. The Advanced checks can take more than an hour and perform checks for enterprise scenarios such as full Active Directory synchronization. You can choose to perform both Quick and Advanced checks as shown in Figure 1-18.

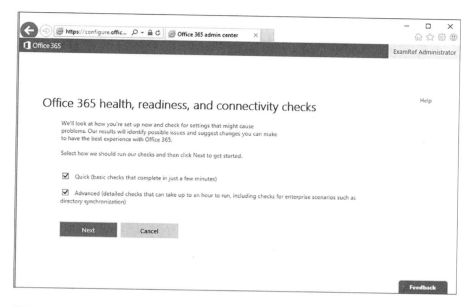

FIGURE 1-18 Quick and Advanced

2. Once you've selected which checks you wish to perform, click Run Checks. This will trigger the download and installation of the Microsoft Office 365 Support Assistant as shown in Figure 1-19.

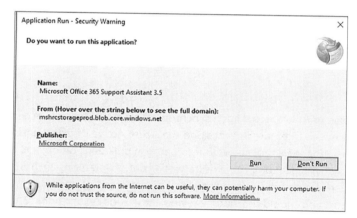

FIGURE 1-19 Office 365 Support Assistant

3. Once installation has occurred, checks will automatically be run to determine the configuration of your environment. Figure 1-20 shows the output of the check where several critical issues related to user attributes have been found.

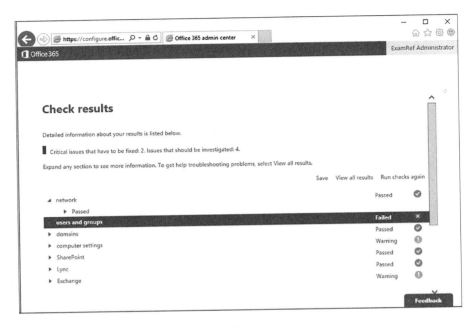

FIGURE 1-20 Health, Readiness, and Connectivity Checks

MORE INFO **OFFICE 365 HEALTH, READINESS AND CONNECTIVITY CHECKS**

You can learn more about the Office 365 on-ramp readiness tool at: *https://support. office.com/en-us/article/Office-365-readiness-checks-c01571b8-183e-4a61-9ca0-80729a48bbda?ui=en-US&rs=en-US&ad=US.*

The IdFix tool

You can use IdFix to resolve most of the common synchronization errors that will occur between an on-premises Active Directory instance and the Azure Active Directory instance used by Office 365. You use the IdFix tool allows you to perform bulk edits on objects that are flagged as likely to have synchronization problems between your on-premises environment and Office 365 prior to performing full synchronization. While IdFix will provide suggestions to resolve the flagged issue, you should thoroughly review these suggestions prior to using IdFix to make changes to existing on-premises Active Directory objects.

MORE INFO **IDFIX TOOL**

You can learn more about the IdFix tool at: *https://www.microsoft.com/en-us/download/ details.aspx?id=36832.*

Create a test plan or use case

Creating a test plan or use case involves developing a formal process to describe how the pilot will proceed and how the results of the pilot will be assessed. The test plan should involve the following general phases:

- Deploying the Office 365 tenancy that will be used for the pilot
- Create user accounts for pilot users
- Configure active use of email for pilot users
- Deploy Office 365 ProPlus software
- Enable pilot user access to Office 365 services
- Solicit pilot user feedback about the experience

Each organization's plans will be slightly different. You need to ensure that pilot user feedback is recorded so that you can use it when evaluating how decisions made in the planning phase stack up against real-world outcomes, allowing you to make adjustments to the deployment phase.

Connect existing email accounts for pilot users

It is possible to migrate the email accounts of a small number of users from your on-premises environment to Office 365 while keeping the majority of your existing mailboxes in the on-premises mail solution. The method for doing this is termed simple domain sharing for SMTP email addresses.

For example:

- Your organization has provisioned the contoso.microsoftonline.com Office 365 tenancy.
- Your organization has its own on-premises mail solution. It uses the contoso.com email suffix.
- Your organization hosts its own DNS records on servers dns1.contoso.com and dns2.contoso.com.
- An MX record in the contoso.com zone points to the host mailserver.adatum.com with a preference of 10.
- An SPF record on in the contoso.com DNS zone the value "v=spf1 mx include:contoso.com -all."

To configure Office 365 so that some pilot users are able to receive email through Office 365 while others still use the on-premises solution, you need to take the following steps:

- Update the SPF record to "v=spf1 mx include:contoso.com include:spf.protection.outlook.com -all."
- Confirm ownership within Office 365 of the contoso.com DNS zone by configuring the appropriate TXT record.

- Mark the domain as shared in Exchange Online. This is done from the mail flow node of Exchange Admin Center as shown in Figure 1-21. Exchange Admin Center is available from the Office 365 Admin Center by clicking the Exchange node under the ADMIN node.

FIGURE 1-21 Mail flow

- You set the domain as an Internal Relay domain as shown in Figure 1-22.

FIGURE 1-22 Internal Relay

- Configure the on-premises mail solution to configure mail forwarding of each pilot user account to the contoso.microsoftonline.com mail domain. For example, the on-premises mailbox for the don.funk@contoso.com email account should forward all incoming email to don.funk@contoso.microsoftonline.com.

- Configure each pilot user's account in Office 365 to use the on-premises DNS zone mail domain. For example, Don Funk's Office 365 user account should be configured with a reply-to address of don.funk@contoso.com.

- You can migrate the contents of pilot users' on-premises mailboxes using Exchange Admin Center.

> **MORE INFO** **PILOT OFFICE 365 EMAIL**
>
> You can learn more about piloting Office 365 email at: *https://support.office.com/en-nz/article/Pilot-Office-365-with-a-few-email-addresses-on-your-custom-domain-39cee536-6a03-40cf-b9c1-f301bb6001d7.*

Service descriptions

Office 365 is made up of multiple separate services. Service descriptions provide information about what the service does. The service descriptions for these Office 365 services are as follows:

- **Office 365 Platform Service** The Office 365 platform combines the Microsoft Office suite of desktop applications with cloud-hosted versions of Microsoft communications and collaboration products. You can find the complete service description at: *https://technet.microsoft.com/en-us/library/jj819274.aspx.*

- **Exchange Online** Exchange online provides the capabilities of an on-premises Microsoft Exchange Server deployment, including access to email, calendar, contacts, and tasks, as a cloud-based service. You can find the complete service description at: *https://technet.microsoft.com/en-us/library/exchange-online-service-description.aspx.*

- **Exchange Online Archiving** A cloud-based archiving solution to assist organizations with meeting their archiving, compliance, regulatory, and e-discovery responsibilities. You can find the complete service description at: *https://technet.microsoft.com/en-us/library/exchange-online-archiving-service-description.aspx.*

- **Exchange Online Protection** A cloud-based email-filtering service that protects against spam and malware. This can also be used to enforce data-loss protection policies. You can find the complete service description at: *https://technet.microsoft.com/en-us/library/exchange-online-protection-service-description.aspx.*

- **SharePoint Online** Provides a cloud-hosted SharePoint deployment. You can find the complete service description at: *https://technet.microsoft.com/en-us/library/sharepoint-online-service-description.aspx.*

- **OneDrive for Business** This is an organization-based personal online storage space hosted in the cloud. You can find the complete service description at: *https://technet. microsoft.com/en-us/library/onedrive-for-business-service-description.aspx.*

- **Skype for Business Online** A hosted communications service that allows instant messaging, file transfer, person-to-person audio/visual communication, and conference hosting. You can find the complete service description at: *https://technet.microsoft.com/ en-us/library/skype-for-business-online-service-description.aspx.*

- **Office Online** This allows you to open and edit Word, Excel, PowerPoint, and OneNote documents in a web browser. You can find the complete service description at: *https://technet.microsoft.com/en-us/library/office-online-service-description.aspx.*

- **Office Applications** A subscription service that provides the most recent version of the Office suite of desktop applications. You can find the complete service description at: *https://technet.microsoft.com/en-us/library/office-applications-service-description. aspx.*

- **Project Online** An online solution for project portfolio management. You can find the complete service description at: *https://technet.microsoft.com/en-us/library/project-online-service-description.aspx.*

- **Project Pro for Office 365** Provides an up-to-date version of the Project Professional software to desktop computers. You can find the complete service description at: *https://technet.microsoft.com/en-us/library/project-pro-for-office-365-service-description.aspx.*

- **Yammer** A cloud-hosted enterprise social network. You can find the complete service description at: *https://technet.microsoft.com/en-us/library/yammer-service-description.aspx.*

- **Power BI for Office 365** An online business intelligence service for managing, sharing, and consuming data queries and Excel workbooks that store data models, queries, and reports. You can find the complete service description at: *https://technet.microsoft. com/en-us/library/power-bi-for-office-365-service-description.aspx.*

- **Microsoft Dynamics CRM Online** Provides online customer relationship management (CRM) capabilities. You can find the complete service description at: *https:// technet.microsoft.com/en-us/library/microsoft-dynamics-crm-online-service-description. aspx.*

MORE INFO **OFFICE 365 SERVICE DESCRIPTIONS**

You can learn more about Office 365 service descriptions at: *https://technet.microsoft.com/ en-us/library/office-365-service-descriptions.aspx.*

FastTrack for Office 365

FastTrack for Office 365 is a set of information tools that assist organizations with planning and migrating to Office 365. For example, FastTrack for Office 365 can assist you with creating a business case for moving to Office 365, perform a self-assessment to determine service readiness, generate Office 365 onboarding plans, as well as generate training regimens so that you can ensure that workers in your organization are ready for the transition to Office 365.

Organizations with more than 50 Office 365 seats can request FastTrack engineering remote support to assist with the migration to Office 365. This includes assistance with migration assessment, pre-migration issue remediation, the migration itself, and a post migration review.

> **MORE INFO** **FASTTRACK FOR OFFICE 365**
>
> You can learn more about FastTrack for Office 365 at: *https://fasttrack.microsoft.com/office.*

EXAM TIP

Remember which record type needs to be modified to allow some pilot users to have email hosted in Office 365 without configuring a hybrid Exchange deployment.

Thought experiment

In this thought experiment, demonstrate your skills and knowledge of the topics covered in this chapter. You can find answers to this thought experiment in the next section.

You have been asked to provide some advice to Fabrikam, a small manufacturing business that migrated to Office 365. Fabrikam needs your advice because the person responsible for Fabrikam's IT recently left the company. During the process, they handed over the credentials of all their Office 365 accounts to the CEO.

The CEO also reports to you that there have been license problems. The company initially purchased a 50-license subscription. Since then, 10 new users have been employed to replace 10 people who left the company over the last few months. The employees who departed still have Office 365 accounts.

Fabrikam has signed up for an Office 365 subscription and is currently using the tenant name Fabrikam.onmicrosoft.com. Fabrikam wants to assign their custom domain, Fabrikam.com, to Office 365 and to have Microsoft DNS servers host this zone. With this information in mind, answer the following questions:

1. What kind of DNS record must be added to confirm ownership of the Fabrikam.com DNS zone?

2. Which DNS records must be modified to have Microsoft DNS servers host the Fabrikam.com DNS zone?

3. Describe the nature of at least one user account that will have global administrator rights for Fabrikam's Office 365 subscription.

4. What methods can be used to resolve the license conflicts?

Thought experiment answers

This section contains the solution to the thought experiment. Each answer explains why the answer choice is correct.

1. A TXT record must be added to confirm ownership of the Fabrikam.com DNS zone.

2. The NS records for the zone must be modified to allow Microsoft to host the Fabrikam.com DNS zone.

3. The first user account created for a subscription will be assigned global administrator privileges. This will be the user account of the IT staff member who recently left and who set up Office 365.

4. The license conflict can be resolved by either manually removing licenses from the 10 users who have left the organization, or by deleting their user accounts.

Chapter summary

- The tenant name is the name that precedes the onmicrosoft.com name for the Office 365 tenancy. This name must be unique.

- While the tenant name can be used as the organization's email domain, you can also configure the tenancy to use a custom email domain for this purpose.

- The first account setup for the tenancy will be assigned the global administrator role.

- Users assigned the global administrator role have access to all administrative features.

- Users assigned the billing administrator role are able to make purchases, manage subscriptions, manage support tickets, and monitor service health.

- Users assigned the password administrator role are able to reset the passwords of most Office 365 user accounts (except those assigned the global admin, service admin, or billing roles).

- Users assigned the service administrator role are able to manage service requests and monitor service health.

- Users assigned the user management admin are able to reset passwords; monitor service health; and manage user accounts, user groups, and service requests.

- You can assign and remove licenses by editing an Office 365 user's properties.

- Deleting a user removes all licenses assigned to that user.

- Pilot users should provide a representative sample of your organization.

- Not all workloads can be or should be migrated to Office 365. Use the pilot phase to determine which workloads you will not migrate.

- A test plan or use case is a document that provides information on each phase of the migration process.

- You can configure pilot users with Office 365 mailboxes through the configuration of SPF records, accepted domains, and email forwarding.

- Office 365 service descriptions provide precise information about Office 365 service functionality.

- Before you can use a custom domain with Office 365, you need to prove that your organization has ownership of the domain.

- You prove to Microsoft that your organization has ownership of a domain by configuring a custom TXT record.

- You can configure MX records for your custom domain to allow mail to be routed to Office 365.

- You can configure CNAME and SRV records to configure the custom domain name to work with Skype for Business (formerly known as Lync).

CHAPTER 2

Plan and implement networking and security in Office 365

If you are using a custom DNS domain with Office 365, you must configure this domain with appropriate DNS records to ensure that your organization's clients are able to find the appropriate Office 365 servers on the Internet. Office 365 requires that clients be able to connect directly to the Office 365 servers on the Internet using a variety of protocols and ports. If the clients cannot make these connections, Office 365 functionality may be limited. As is the case with on-premises Active Directory, Office 365 supports different administrative roles. In large organizations, these roles can be used to allow IT staff, such as those that work on the service desk, to perform support tasks without being granted unnecessary privileges.

Skills in this chapter:

- Configure DNS records for services
- Enable client connectivity to Office 365
- Administer Microsoft Azure Rights Management
- Manage administrator roles in Office 365

Skill 2.1: Configure DNS records for services

This skill deals with the configuration of DNS records in custom DNS domains, allowing those domains to be used with Office 365 services. To master this skill you'll need to understand the types of records needed to be added to a custom DNS domain to support Exchange, Skype for Business, and SharePoint Online.

> **This section covers the following topics:**
> - Exchange DNS records
> - Skype for Business Online DNS records
> - SharePoint Online DNS records
> - Update and verify DNS records for Office 365 settings

Exchange DNS records

When you provision Office 365 for your organization, Microsoft takes care of ensuring that the DNS records for your organization's tenant domain, which is the onmicrosoft.com domain, are configured properly so that email addresses that use the tenant domain as an email domain suffix have mail routed properly.

For example, if you provision an Office 365 tenant and the tenant domain is contoso. onmicrosoft.com, then email sent to users at this email domain, such as an email sent to don.funk@contoso.onmicrosoft.com, will arrive at the correct location because Office 365 will provision the appropriate DNS records automatically when the tenancy is provisioned.

When you add a custom domain to Office 365, you need to configure an appropriate set of DNS records to ensure that mail flows properly to Office 365 mailboxes that use the custom domain. For example, if your custom domain is tailspintoys.com, you need to configure DNS so that email will function properly for Office 365 mailboxes that are configured to use the tailspintoys.com email domain. When properly configured, the user associated with the Office 365 mailbox don.funk@tailspintoys.com will receive email sent from other hosts on the Internet.

As you learned in "Chapter 1: Provision Office 365," if your custom DNS zone is hosted by GoDaddy, Office 365 can configure the appropriate DNS records for you automatically. If your custom DNS zone is hosted by another DNS hosting provider, you'll have to configure DNS records manually.

You need to configure the following DNS records:
- Autodiscover CNAME record for Autodiscover service
- MX record for mail routing
- SPF (Sender Policy Framework) record to verify identity of mail server
- TXT record for Exchange federation
- CNAME record for Exchange federation

Autodiscover CNAME record

You need to create a CNAME record that uses the Autodiscover alias to point to the hostname Autodiscover.outlook.com so that Outlook clients have their settings automatically provisioned for Office 365. For example, if the custom domain you assigned to Office 365 was tailspintoys.com, you would need to create the CNAME record Autodiscover.tailspintoys.com and have it point to Autodiscover.outlook.com. Figure 2-1 shows this type of record being created in the DNS console of a DNS server running the Windows Server 2012 R2 operating system.

FIGURE 2-1 Autodiscover record

MX record

You need to configure an MX record in your custom domain to point to an Office 365 target mail server. The address of this target mail server will depend on the name of the custom domain and is described in the documentation as being in the form <mx token>.mail.protection.outlook.com. You can determine the value for MX token by performing the following steps:

1. In the Office 365 Admin Center, navigate to the Domains node under Settings.
2. Select the custom domain; this will open the Domain properties page.
3. Locate the MX record as shown in Figure 2-2.

FIGURE 2-2 Autodiscover record

To ensure that mail routes properly, you need to configure the MX priority for the record to be a lower value than any other MX records configured for the custom domain. When mail is being routed, a check is performed to determine which MX record has the lowest value for the priority field. For example, an MX record with a priority of 10 will be chosen as a destination for mail routing over an MX record with a priority of 20.

Figure 2-3 shows the MX record for the tailspintoys.com custom domain. The mail server priority is set to 10 and the MX token is tailspintoys-com.

FIGURE 2-3 MX record

SPF record

The Sender Protection Framework (SPF) record is a special TXT record that reduces the possibility of malicious third parties using the custom domain to send spam or malicious email. An SPF record is used to validate which email servers are authorized to send messages on behalf of the custom domain. The SPF record must be a TXT record where the TXT value must include **v=spf1 include:spf.protection.outlook.com –all**. The record should also be set with a TTL value of **3600**. Figure 2-4 shows an SPF record for Office 365 created in the DNS console for Windows Server 2012 R2 where the tailspintoys.com custom domain is being used.

FIGURE 2-4 SPF record

> **MORE INFO SPF RECORDS**
>
> You can learn more about DNS records for Exchange in Office 365 at: *https://support.office. com/en-in/article/External-Domain-Name-System-records-for-Office-365-c0531a6f-9e25- 4f2d-ad0e-a70bfef09ac0.*

Exchange federation TXT records

If you are configuring federation between an on-premises Exchange deployment and Office 365, you need to create two special TXT records that will include a custom-generated domain-proof hash text.

The first record will include the custom domain name and the hash text, such as tailspintoys.com and Y96nu89138789315669824, respectively. The second record will include the name exchangedelegation with the custom domain name and then the custom generated domain-proof hash text like exchangedelegation.tailspintoys.com and Y3259071352452626169.

Exchange federation CNAME record

If you are configuring federation, you need an additional CNAME record to support federation with Office 365. This CNAME record will need the alias autodiscover.service and should also point to autodiscover.outlook.com. Figure 2-5 shows the configuration of this record for the tailspintoys.com domain on a DNS server running the Windows Server 2012 R2 operating system.

FIGURE 2-5 Autodiscover record

> **MORE INFO DNS RECORDS FOR EXCHANGE IN OFFICE 365**
>
> You can learn more about DNS records for Exchange in Office 365 at: *https://support.office. com/en-in/article/External-Domain-Name-System-records-for-Office-365-c0531a6f-9e25- 4f2d-ad0e-a70bfef09ac0.*

Skype for Business Online DNS records

Skype for Business requires you to configure two types of DNS records if you have a custom domain. You need to configure two SRV records and two CNAME records to get Skype for Business working properly. Figure 2-6 shows the Skype for Business Online records needed for the contoso2017er.com domain.

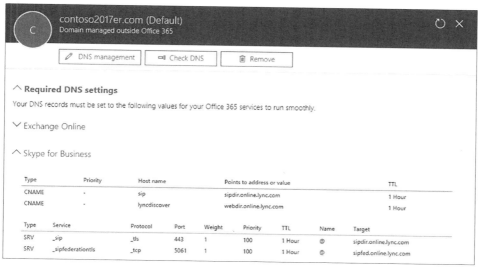

FIGURE 2-6 Skype for Business DNS records

Skype for Business Online SRV records

Skype for Business Online requires two SRV records. The first record is used to coordinate the flow of data between Skype for Business clients. This record should have the following properties:

- Service: **_sip**
- Protocol: **_TCP**
- Priority: **100**
- Weight: **1**
- Port: **443**
- Target: **sipdir.online.lync.com**

An example of this record created in the DNS console on a computer running Windows Server 2012 R2 for the tailspintoys.com custom domain is shown in Figure 2-7.

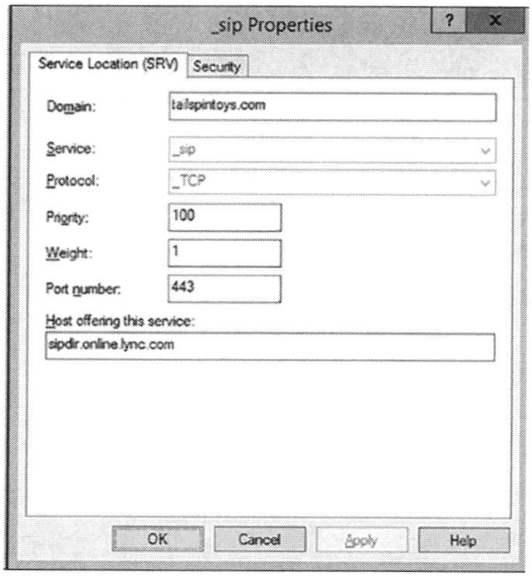

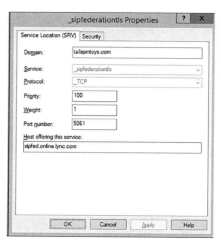

FIGURE 2-7 SRV record

The second record is used by Skype for Business to share instant messaging features with clients other than Lync for Business by allowing SIP federation. This record should have the following properties:

- Service: **_sipfederationtls**
- Protocol: **_TCP**
- Priority: **100**
- Weight: **1**
- Port: **5061**
- Target: **sipfed.online.lync.com**

This record, configured for the tailspintoys.com custom domain, is shown in Figure 2-8.

FIGURE 2-8 SRV record for federation

Skype for Business Online CNAME records

If you want to use Skype for Business with a custom domain, you also need to create two separate CNAME records. The first CNAME record uses the alias sip and points to sipdir.online. lync.com. This CNAME record allows the client to find the Skype for Business service and assists in the process of signing in. A version of this record, created for the tailspintoys.com custom domain, is shown in Figure 2-9.

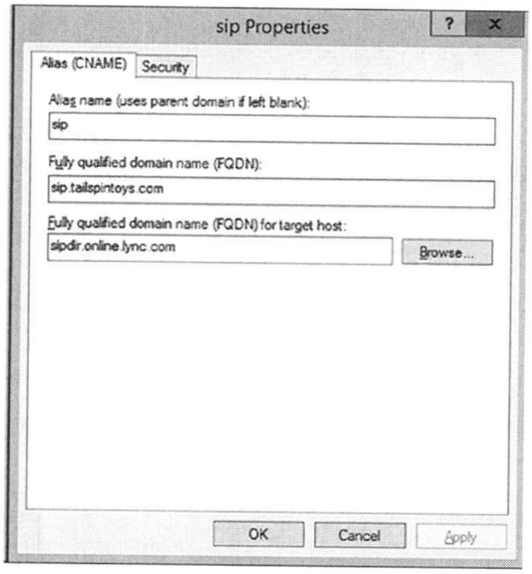

FIGURE 2-9 CNAME record

The second CNAME record assists the Skype for Business mobile device client to find the Skype for Business service and also assists with sign-in. The alias for this record is lyncdiscover and the record target is webdir.online.lync.com. An example of this record for the custom domain tailspintoys.com is shown in Figure 2-10.

FIGURE 2-10 CNAME for Skype for Business

MORE INFO SKYPE FOR BUSINESS

You can learn more about setting up DNS records for Skype for Business at: *https://support.office.microsoft.com/en-us/article/Set-up-your-network-for-Skype-for-Business-Online-81fa5e16-418d-4698-a5f0-e666211c5c66.*

SharePoint Online DNS records

You only have to configure a DNS record in a custom domain for SharePoint Online if you are going to allow SharePoint Online to send email to people outside your organization. If you are doing this, you'll need to update the SPF record that you configured for your custom domain to include the text include:sharepointonline.com. For example, Figure 2-11 shows the SPF record configured for the tailspintoys.com DNS zone modified to now include the value include:sharepointonline.com.

FIGURE 2-11 SharePoint Online SPF modification

MORE INFO SPF RECORDS FOR SHAREPOINT ONLINE

You can learn more about configuring SPF records for SharePoint Online at: *https://support.office.com/en-in/article/External-Domain-Name-System-records-for-Office-365-c0531a6f-9e25-4f2d-ad0e-a70bfef09ac0.*

Update and verify DNS records for Office 365 settings

You can verify that DNS records have been configured correctly by using the Check DNS button, located in the DNS domain page as shown in Figure 2-12.

FIGURE 2-12 Verify DNS records

Skill 2.2: Enable client connectivity to Office 365

This skill deals with enabling client connectivity to Office 365 servers on the Internet. To master this skill you'll need to understand how to configure a proxy server to allow anonymous access to Office 365, how to configure outbound firewalls to allow traffic to pass on the appropriate ports, understand which tools to use to calculate Office 365 bandwidth requirements, understand common client Internet connectivity problems, and how to configure previous versions of Office clients to connect to Office 365.

This section covers the following topics:
- Proxy server configuration
- Outbound firewall ports
- Recommend bandwidth
- Internet connectivity for clients
- Deploy desktop setup for previous versions of Office clients

Proxy server configuration

Clients are unable to make connections to Office 365 if their Internet traffic passes through a proxy server that requires authentication. If your organization has a proxy server that requires authentication, you must either choose to disable authentication entirely, or selectively disable authentication for traffic to Office 365 related resources on the Internet.

The number of URLs that you need to configure for exclusion is substantial and a complete list is beyond the scope of this book. The URLs and IP address ranges that are associated with Office 365 are always changing, and it is possible to subscribe to an RSS feed that will provide notification when URLs and IP addresses change.

Outbound firewall ports

Clients need to be able to make connections to the Office 365 servers on the Internet using certain protocols and ports. If certain ports and protocols are blocked by a perimeter network firewall, clients will be unable to use specific Office 365 services. Table 2-1 lists the protocols and ports that need to be open for clients on an internal network to hosts on the Internet.

TABLE 2-1: Office 365 Outbound Port requirements

Protocol	Port	Used by
TCP	443	■ Office 365 portal ■ Outlook ■ Outlook Web App ■ SharePoint Online ■ Skype for Business client ■ ADFS Federation ■ ADFS Proxy
TCP	25	Mail routing
TCP	587	SMTP relay
TCP	143/993	IMAP Simple Migration Tool
TCP	80/443	■ Microsoft Azure Active Directory Sync tool ■ Exchange Management Console ■ Exchange Management Shell
TCP	995	POP3 secure
PSOM/TLS	443	Skype for Business Online: Outbound data sharing
STUN/TCP	443	Skype for Business Online: Outbound audio, video, and application sharing sessions
STUN/UDP	3478	Skype for Business Online: Outbound audio and video sessions
TCP	5223	Skype for Business mobile client push notifications
UDP	20000-45000	Skype for Business Online outbound phone
RTC/UDP	50000-59000	Skype for Business Online: Outbound audio and video sessions.

Recommend bandwidth

There are many factors that influence the amount of bandwidth that an organization will require to successfully use Office 365. These factors include:

- The specific Office 365 services to which the organization has subscribed.
- The number of clients connecting to Office 365 from a site at any point in time.
- The type of interaction the client is having with Office 365.
- The performance of the Internet browser software on each client computer.
- The capacity of the network connection available to each client computer.
- Your organization's network topology.

Microsoft provides a number of tools that can be used to estimate the bandwidth requirements of an Office 365 deployment. These include:

- **Exchange Client Network Bandwidth Calculator**   This tool allows you to estimate the bandwidth required for Outlook, Outlook Web App, and mobile device users.
- **Skype for Business Online Bandwidth Calculator**   This tool allows you to estimate the amount of bandwidth you will require based on the number of Skype for Business users and the specific features those users will be leveraging.
- **OneDrive for Business Synchronization Calculator**   This tool provides network bandwidth estimates based on how users use OneDrive for Business.

Internet connectivity for clients

To use Office 365, clients need to be able to establish unauthenticated connections over port 80 and port 443 to the Office 365 servers on the Internet. On some networks, especially those configured for small businesses, you may run into the following network connectivity problems:

- **Clients configured with APIPA addresses**   If clients are configured with IP addresses in the APIPA range (169.254.0.0 /16), they most likely cannot make a connection to the Internet. They should be configured with IP addresses in the private range with an appropriate default gateway configured to connect either directly or indirectly to the Internet.

- **No default gateway**   Clients need to be configured with a default gateway address of a device that can route traffic to the Internet. The default gateway device doesn't need to be directly connected to the Internet, but it needs to be able to route traffic to a device that eventually does connect to the Internet.

- **Firewall configuration**   Clients require access to the Internet on the ports outlined earlier in the chapter.

- **Proxy server authentication**   Office 365 does not work if an intervening proxy server requires authentication for connections. You'll have to configure an authentication bypass for Office 365 addresses, or disable proxy server authentication.

Deploy desktop setup for previous versions of Office clients

Versions of Office prior to Office 2007, such as Office 2003, needed special configuration to work with Office 365. Office 2003 extended support expired on the same date that Windows XP extended support expired in April 2014. It is important to note that Office 2007 support ends in October 2017.

At the time of writing, Office 2007 is supported with Office 365. For example, Outlook 2007 supports configuration through the Autodiscover protocol, which means that it is possible to configure Outlook 2007 by providing an Office 365 username and password, just as it is possible to configure Outlook 2010 and Outlook 2013 in this manner.

> **MORE INFO** **USING OFFICE 2007 WITH OFFICE 365**
>
> You can learn more about configuring Outlook 2007 for Office 365 at: *https://support. office.com/en-us/article/Set-up-email-in-Outlook-2007-1cf5c44a-43c1-4332-bb54-0d7545322cc0.*

EXAM TIP

Remember that clients will be unable to access Office 365 if client traffic passes through a proxy server that requires authentication.

Skill 2.3: Administer Microsoft Azure Rights Management

This skill deals with rights management in Office 365, which allows you to control who is able to access information and the tasks that they can perform with that information. Allowing someone to open a document, but to not modify that document or copy the contents of that document is an example. To master this skill you'll need to understand the basics of rights management, how Microsoft Office integrates with rights management, the roles for Microsoft Azure Active Directory rights management, and how to recover a protected document.

This section covers the following topics:

- Activate rights management
- Office integration with rights management
- Assign roles for Microsoft Azure Active Directory RM
- Enable recovery of protected document
- Setup templates for rights management protected email

Azure Information Protection

One issue that often causes confusion is the way that Microsoft names certain technologies, specifically the more recently released Azure Information Protection. This leads many people to wonder if Azure Information Protection is the replacement technology for Azure Rights Management.

Azure Information Protection is not the replacement for Azure Rights Management. Azure Rights Management functions as the underlying protection technology used by Azure Information Protection (AIP). This skill will likely eventually be renamed to Azure Information Protection in the future.

MORE INFO **ALSO KNOWN AS**

In an attempt to explain the difference and overlap between Azure Information Protection and Azure Rights Management, Microsoft has provided the following document: *https://docs.microsoft.com/en-us/information-protection/understand-explore/aka.*

Activate Azure Rights Management and Azure Information Protection

Azure Information Protection leverages Azure Rights Management to provide Office 365 subscribers with the ability to control how documents are consumed and who can access those documents, even if they are inadvertently sent to unauthorized third parties. Azure Information Protection isn't enabled by default on Office 365 subscriptions and does attract additional per user charges once activated.

To activate Azure Information Protection and Azure Rights Management, ensure thatperform the following steps:

1. Ensure that you are signed into the Office 365 Admin Center with an account that has global administrator permissions.

2. In the Office 365 Admin Center, in the Settings section, click Microsoft Azure Information Protection and then click Manage Microsoft Azure Information Protection Settings.

3. On the Rights Management page, shown in Figure 2-13, click Activate. The Office 365 interface at this point switches from using the term Azure Information Protection to using Azure Rights Management. At some point, this discontinuity is likely to be resolved.

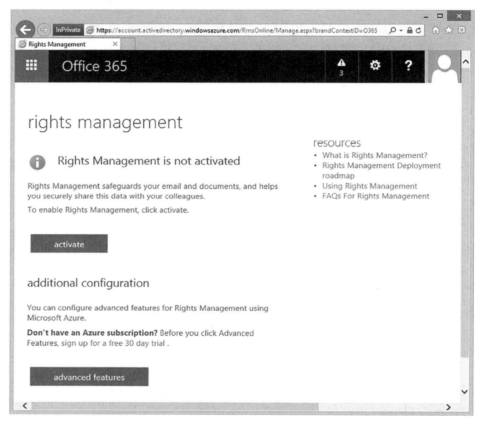

FIGURE 2-13 Active Rights Management

4. On the Do You Want To Activate Rights Management page, shown in Figure 2-14, click Activate.

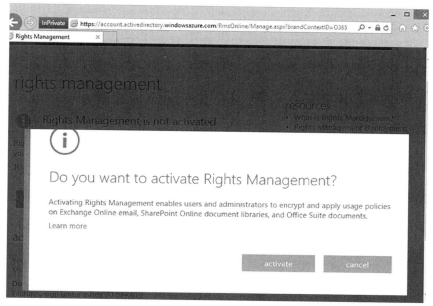

FIGURE 2-14 Do You Want To Activate Rights Management

5. After a few minutes, the message that Rights Management is activated will be displayed, as shown in Figure 2-15.

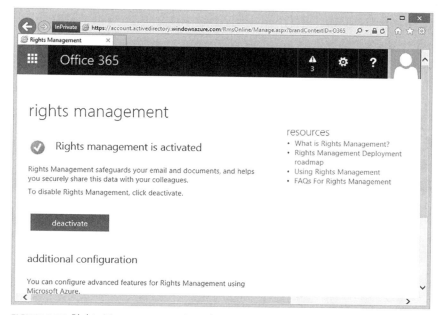

FIGURE 2-15 Rights Management activated

You can enable or disable Rights Management services for your organization using the Enable-Aadrm and Disable-Aadrm cmdlets that are part of the AADRM PowerShell module.

> **MORE INFO** **ACTIVATE AZURE RIGHTS MANAGEMENT**
>
> You can learn more about activating Azure Information Protection (Azure Rights Management) at: *https://docs.microsoft.com/en-us/information-protection/deploy-use/activate-service.*

Office integration with Rights Management

It is necessary for users wishing to use Azure Information Protection to be signed into Office 365 from the Office product that they want to configure with Rights Management. A user can verify that they are signed into Office 365 by checking their account information. Figure 2-16 shows the account information for a user signed into Word with their Office 365 user account.

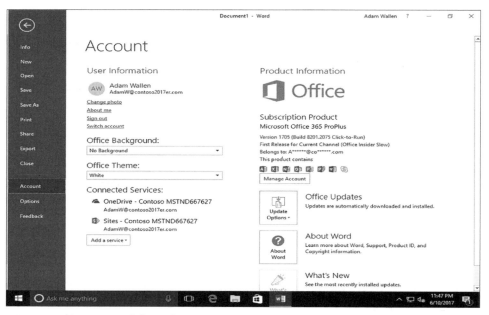

FIGURE 2-16 User account information

Once a user is signed in, they will have access to the Protect Document menu on the Info page of the Stage menu as shown in Figure 2-17.

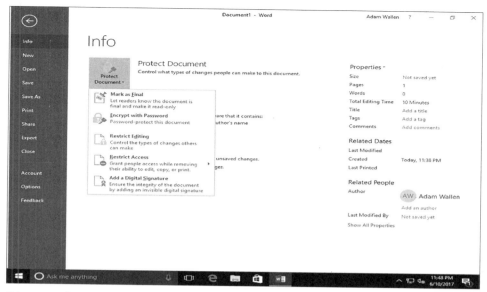

FIGURE 2-17 Protect Document

It may be necessary to connect to the Azure Rights Management servers to get templates. This can be done by clicking Restrict Access and then clicking Connect To Rights Management Servers and Get Templates as shown in Figure 2-18.

FIGURE 2-18 Restrict Access

Once the templates have been retrieved from the server, these organization specific templates will be visible in the Restrict Access menu, as shown in Figure 2-19.

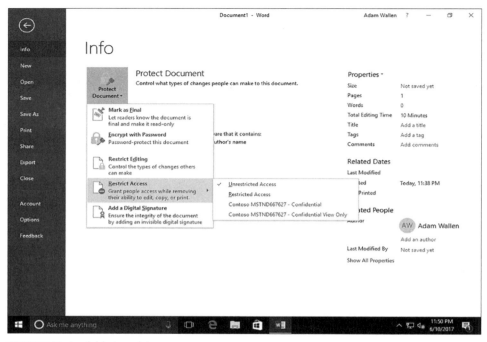

FIGURE 2-19 Available templates

> **MORE INFO CONFIGURE APPLICATIONS FOR AZURE RIGHTS MANAGEMENT**
>
> You can learn more about configuring applications for Azure Rights Management at:
> *https://docs.microsoft.com/en-us/information-protection/deploy-use/configure-applications.*

Assign roles for Microsoft Azure Active Directory RM

Azure Rights Management administrators are able to control the Azure Rights Management service, but are unable to view data protected by the service. You can add a user or group as an Azure Rights Management administrator using the Add-AadrmRoleBasedAdministrator cmdlet.

The Azure Rights Management super user feature allows authorized people and services to view the data that is protected by the Azure Rights Management Service. An Azure Rights Management super user is able to modify the protection applied to a protected document. An Azure Rights Management super user is able to:

- Access documents protected by a user that has left the organization.
- Alter the protection policy applied to existing files.

- Be configured to allow Exchange Server to index mailboxes containing protected content.
- Be configured to allow Data Loss Prevention products and anti-malware products to scan protected documents.
- Perform bulk decryption of files for auditing, legal, or compliance reasons.

The Azure Rights Management super user feature is not enabled by default. It will be enabled automatically when the Rights Management connector is configured for Exchange Server. A user who is configured as an Azure Rights Management administrator can enable the super user role and add users to this role, but cannot by themselves access the protected content unless their account is a member of this role.

You enable the Azure Rights Management super user role using the Enable-Aadrm-SuperUserFeature cmdlet. You can add user and service accounts to this role using the Add-AadrmSuperUser cmdlet. You can only add individual accounts to the super user role, you can't add security groups to this role. You can disable the super user feature using the Disable-AadrmSuperUserFeature cmdlet. You can view which users have been assigned Azure Rights Management super user privileges using the Get-AadrmSuperUser cmdlet.

> **MORE INFO AZURE ACTIVE DIRECTORY ROLES**
>
> You can learn more about Azure Active Directory Roles at: *https://technet.microsoft.com/en-us/library/mt147272.aspx.*

Enable recovery of protected document

A user that has been assigned Azure Rights Management super user role is able to remove protection from a document using the Unprotect-RMSFile cmdlet. A user that has these privileges is able to re-apply Rights Management protection using the Protect-RMSFile cmdlet.

Configure rights management email templates

At present, while you manage most Azure Information Protection features from the new Azure portal, you actually configure templates for rights management from the classic portal. This is likely to change in the future as all Azure functionality becomes available in the new Azure portal.

To configure a template for rights management protected email, perform the following steps:

1. In the Azure classic portal, click Active Directory and then click Rights Management. This will open the Rights Management page shown in Figure 2-20.

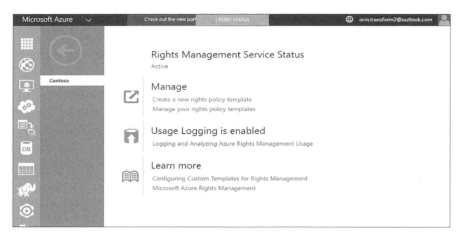

FIGURE 2-20 Manage Templates

2. To view existing templates, click on Manage your rights policy templates. When Azure Information Protection is enabled, two policies, Confidential and Confidential View Only, are automatically created as shown in Figure 2-21.

FIGURE 2-21 Default Templates

3. To create a new template, click Add.

4. On the Add A New Rights Policy Template page, add a name for the template, specify a language, and provide a description. Once the template is created, click on the template to edit the properties of that template.

5. On the Rights page, specify which users or groups the template will apply to. Figure 2-22 shows the All Employees group selected.

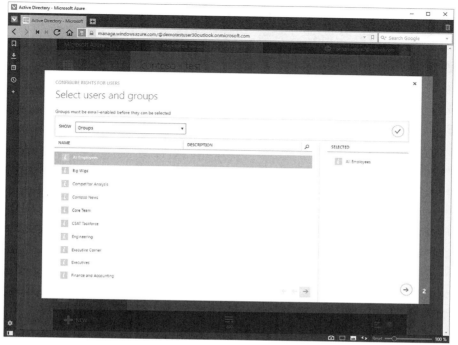

FIGURE 2-22 Template users and groups

6. On the User and Group Rights page, select which rights apply to the group. You can choose between the following:

- **Viewer** Grants the View, Reply, and Reply All permissions.
- **Reviewer** Grants the View, Edit, Reply, Reply All and Forward permissions.
- **Co-Author** Grants the View, Edit, Copy, Print, Reply, Reply All and Forward permissions.
- **Co-Owner** Grants all available rights.
- **Custom** Allows rights to be granted selectively. Custom rights are shown in Figure 2-23.

FIGURE 2-23 Custom rights

7. On the Scope tab, specify which users will be able to apply the template. By default, all users in an organization can apply a template.

8. On the Configure tab, shown in Figure 2-24, you can choose whether to publish or archive the template, which languages the template can be used with, the content expiration settings, and whether content protected by the template can be viewed offline.

FIGURE 2-24 Template configuration

Managing Azure Rights Management using PowerShell

You can manage Azure Rights Management using cmdlets in the AADRM module, which you can obtain by downloading the Azure Rights Management Administration Tool from the Microsoft Download Center. Table 2-2 lists the cmdlets that you can use to perform specific tasks.

TABLE 2-2. AADRM tasks and associated cmdlets

Task	Associated cmdlets
Connect and disconnect to AADRM	Connect-AadrmService Disconnect-Aadrmservice
Create and manage rights management templates	Add-AadrmTemplate Export-AadrmTemplate Get-AadrmTemplate Get-AadrmTemplateProperty Import-AadrmTemplate New-AadrmRightsDefinition Remove-AadrmTemplate Set-AadrmTemplateProperty
Configure use license validity period	Set-AadrmMaxUseLicenseValidityTime Get-AadrmMaxUseLicenseValidityTime
View Rights Management Service Configuration	Get-AadrmConfiguration

EXAM TIP

Remember which cmdlet you use to add users to the Azure Rights Management super user role and which cmdlet enables the role.

Skill 2.4: Manage administrator roles in Office 365

This skill deals with the different administrator roles that are available in Office 365. In Chapter 1, you learned basic information about some of these roles. To master this skill you'll need to understand the differences between each of the roles, and understand how you can assign and revoke role membership.

> **This section covers the following topics:**
> - Global administrator
> - Billing administrator
> - User management administrator
> - Service administrator
> - Password administrator
> - Delegated administrator
> - Exchange administrator
> - Skype for Business administrator
> - SharePoint administrator
> - Manage role membership

Global administrator

As you learned in the previous chapter, global administrators have the most permissions over an Office 365 tenancy. A global administrator has the following permissions:

- View organization and user information
- Manage support tickets
- Reset user passwords
- Perform billing and purchasing operations
- Create and manage user views
- Create, edit, and delete users
- Create, edit, and delete groups
- Manage user licenses
- Manage domains
- Manage organization information
- Delegate administrative roles to others
- User directory synchronization

Users that have the global administrator role in the Office 365 tenancy have the following roles in Exchange Online:

- Exchange Online admin
- Company admin
- SharePoint Online admin
- Skype for Business Online admin

> **MORE INFO** **GLOBAL ADMINISTRATOR ROLE**
>
> You can learn more about the global administrator role at: *https://support.office.com/en-us/article/About-Office-365-admin-roles-da585eea-f576-4f55-a1e0-87090b6aaa9d*.

Billing administrator

Members of the billing administrator role are responsible for making purchases, managing Office 365 subscriptions, managing support tickets, and monitoring the health of Office 365 services. Members of the billing administrator role have the following permissions:

- View organization and user information
- Manage support tickets
- Perform billing and purchasing operations

Members of this role do not have any equivalent roles in Exchange Online, SharePoint Online, or Skype for Business Online.

User management administrator

Members of the user management administrator role are able to reset some user passwords, monitor service health, manage some user accounts, and groups, and service requests. Members of this role have the following permissions:

- View organization and user information
- Manage support tickets
- Reset the passwords of all user accounts except those assigned the global administrator, billing administrator, or service administrator roles
- Create and manage user views
- Can create, edit, and delete users and groups except users that are assigned global administrator privileges
- Can manage user licenses
- Have the Skype for Business Online admin role

Service administrator

Members of the service administrator role are able to manage service requests and monitor the health of services. Before a global administrator can assign the service administrator role to a user, the user must be assigned administrative permissions to one of the Office 365 services, such as SharePoint Online or Exchange Online. Service administrators have the following permissions over the assigned service:

- View organization and user information
- Manage support tickets

Password administrator

Members of the password administrator role are responsible for resetting passwords for non-privileged users and other members of the password administrator role. Members of this role are also able to manage service requests and monitor service health. Members of this role have the following permissions:

- View organization and user information.
- Manage support tickets.
- Can reset non-privileged user passwords as well as passwords of other password administrators. Cannot reset passwords of global administrators, user management administrators, or billing administrators.
- Manage the Exchange Online Help Desk admin role.
- Manage the Skype for Business Online admin role.

Delegated administrator

Delegated administrators are people outside the organization that perform administrative duties within the Office 365 tenancy. Administrators of the tenancy control who has delegated administrator permissions. You can only assign delegated administrator permissions to users that have Office 365 accounts in their own tenancy.

When you configure delegated administration, you can choose one of the following permission levels:

- **Full administration**   When you assign the full administration role to a delegated administrator, that administrator has the same privileges as a member of the global admin role.
- **Limited administration**   When you assign the limited administration role to a delegated administrator, that administrator has the same privileges as a member of the password admin role.

Exchange Online administrator

Users delegated the Exchange Online administrator role are able to manage mailboxes and anti-spam policies for your tenancy. This includes being able to:

- Recover deleted items from mailboxes
- Configure how long deleted items will be retained before permanent deletion
- Configure mailbox sharing policies
- Configure Send As and Send on Behalf of delegates for a mailbox
- Configure anti-spam and malware filters
- Create shared mailboxes.

Skype for Business administrator

Users delegated the Skype for Business administrator role are able to perform the following tasks:

- Set up dial-in conferencing
- Set up PSTN calling
- Transfer phone numbers to Skype for Business Online
- Enable Skype Meeting Broadcast
- Allow users to contact external Skype for Business users
- Allow users to add external contacts from Skype
- Determine who is able to view online presence
- Enable and disable mobile notifications
- Create customized meeting invitations
- View Skype for Business Online online activity reports

SharePoint Online administrator

Users delegated the SharePoint Online administrator role are able to use the SharePoint Online admin center. They are able to perform the following tasks:

- Create and manage site collections
- Manage site collections and global settings
- Designate site collection administrators
- Manage site collection storage limits
- Manage SharePoint online user profiles

Manage role membership

You can assign an administrative role on the Edit user roles page of an Office 365 user's properties as shown in Figure 2-25. When you assign an administrative role, you specify the role that you want to assign and an alternate email address allows assigned the role to perform password recovery. You can only add Office 365 users to a role. You cannot add an Office 365 group to a role.

FIGURE 2-25 Password administrator

You can use this page of a user's account to remove an assigned role. To do this, deselect the role that you want to remove and select the No option and then click Save. You can view a list of users assigned a particular role by using the Active Users node in the Office 365 Admin Center and selecting the role whose membership you wish to view. Figure 2-26 shows the members of the password admins role.

FIGURE 2-26 List of password administrators

You can use the following Windows PowerShell cmdlets to manage Office 365 administrative roles:

- **Add-MsolRoleMember**   Add a user to a role
- **Remove-MsolRoleMember**   Remove a user from a role
- **Get-MsolRole**   Retrieve a list of administrative roles
- **Get-MsolRoleMember**   List the members of a specific administrative role

EXAM TIP

Remember the PowerShell cmdlets that you use to manage administrative role membership.

Thought experiment

In this thought experiment, apply what you've learned about this objective. You can find the answers to these questions in the "Answers" section at the end of the chapter.

You are in the process of configuring networking and security at Tailspin toys. This involves configuring SRV records in the tailspintoys.com custom domain to support Skype for Business at Tailspin Toys. You also need to ascertain the bandwidth requirements of a potential Office 365 deployment.

To ensure that Tailspin Toys' intellectual property is protected, you also want to investigate Azure Rights Management. You want to know about how it might be possible for an authorized person to remove rights management protection from a document. You are also interested in learning about managing the super users functionality.

In terms of configuring administrative role membership at Tailspin Toys, you want to allow Sam to create new Office 365 users, but he shouldn't be able to modify administrative roles. You want Don to be able to pay the Office 365 bills, but he shouldn't be assigned any other unnecessary permissions.

With all of this information in mind, answer the following questions:

1. Which port should the _sipfederationtls SRV record be configured to use?
2. Which port should the _sip SRV record be configured to use?
3. Which tool should you use to estimate Skype for Business bandwidth requirements?
4. Which tool should you use to estimate OneDrive for Business bandwidth requirements?
5. Which Windows PowerShell cmdlet removes Azure Rights Management protection?
6. Which Windows PowerShell cmdlet disables the Azure Rights Management super user functionality?
7. Which role should you add Sam to?
8. Which role should you add Don to?

Thought experiment answers

This section contains the solution to the thought experiment. Each answer explains why the answer choice is correct.

1. The _sipfederationtls SRV record should be configured to use TCP port 5061.]

2. Which port should the _sip SRV record be configured to use? [The _sip SRV record should be configured to use TCP port 443.

3. You should use the Skype for Business bandwidth calculator to estimate Skype for Business bandwidth requirements.

4. You should use the OneDrive for Business Synchronization calculator to estimate OneDrive for Business bandwidth requirements

5. The Unprotect-RMSFile cmdlet will remove Azure Rights Management protection from a file.

6. The Disable-AadrmSuperUserFeature cmdlet will disable the Azure Rights Management super user functionality.

7. You should add Sam to the user management administrator role.

8. You should add Don to the billing administrator role.

Chapter summary

- If you are using a custom domain with Office 365, you will need to manually configure certain DNS records in the custom domain.

- The configuration of DNS records in custom DNS domains can be configured to occur automatically if an organization has its DNS zones hosted on GoDaddy.

- Exchange DNS records that require configuration include a CNAME record for Autodiscover, an MX record for mail routing, and an SPF record for spam protection.

- Skype for Business requires that SRV and CNAME records be configured in the custom DNS domains.

- If sending email to external users from SharePoint Online, the SPF record will need to be updated with SharePoint specific information.

- Office 365 does not work if proxy servers between the client and the Office 365 servers require authentication.

- A variety of outbound firewall ports must be open between the client and the Office 365 servers for all Office 365 functionality to be available.

- Microsoft provides a number of tools that can be used to estimate the client bandwidth requirements.

- Clients must be able to connect to the Internet to use Office 365.

- Azure Rights Management isn't activated by default on Office 365 tenancies and must be enabled in the Office 365 Admin Center.

- Office 365 users must be signed in to Office 365 from Office applications before they are able to access Azure Rights Management functionality.

- Azure Rights Management Administrators are able to control the Azure Rights Management Service, but are unable to view data protected by Azure Rights Management.

- Azure Rights Management super users are able to access protected content, as well as modify protection settings applied to documents.

- Azure Rights Management super user functionality must be manually enabled.

- Users that have Azure Rights Management super user permissions can remove protection from a document using the Unprotect-RMSFile Windows PowerShell cmdlet.

- Global administrators have full permissions over an Office 365 tenancy.

- Billing administrators can manage subscriptions, support tickets and monitor tenancy health.

- User management administrators can manage user accounts, but cannot modify the properties of users that are members of administrator groups.

- Service administrators are able to manage service requests and can monitor service health for services that they have been granted permission over.

- Password administrators can reset passwords of non-privileged users.

- Delegated administrators are users from other Office 365 tenancies that have been granted administrator access over the tenancy. They can be assigned global administrator or password administrator permissions.

- Administrator roles can be managed through the Office 365 console or by using the Add-MsolRoleMember, Remove-MsolRoleMember, Get-MsolRole, and Get-MsolRole-Member cmdlets.

CHAPTER 3

Manage cloud identities

Cloud identities is the term used to refer to Office 365 user accounts. These accounts are stored within Azure Active Directory. Users authenticate against Azure Active Directory when signing on to the Office 365 portal or when required to authenticate to use other Office 365 resources. Just as you need to be able to manage user accounts, password policies, and security groups when managing an on-premises environment where users authenticate against Active Directory Domain Controllers, the 70-346 exam requires you to know how to manage Office 365 user accounts, password policies, and security groups using both the Office 365 admin center as well as Windows PowerShell.

Skills in this chapter:

- Configure password management
- Manage user and security groups
- Manage cloud identities with Windows PowerShell

Skill 3.1: Configure password management

This skill deals with configuring the properties of passwords for users of Office 365. Password policies allow you to configure the number of days that needs to elapse before a user's password expires, number of days prior to expiry before a warning is sent, and allows you to set rules about how complex a password must be. This skill also deals with resetting both user account and administrator passwords.

> **This section covers the following topics:**
> - Expiry policy
> - Password complexity
> - Password resets

Working with cloud identities

Cloud identities, including Office 365 user accounts and security groups, are stored within Azure AD rather than in a separate Office 365 specific account database. This means that user identities are subject to Azure Active Directory policies, such as the Azure Active Directory password and account lockout policies. A big adjustment for administrators of traditional on-premises environments is that many settings, such as how complex a password must be, the number of incorrect password entries that trigger a lockout, and the account lockout duration, are configured by Microsoft and cannot be configured by administrators of Office 365 through the Office 365 Admin Center. When studying for the 70-346 exam, candidates need to be familiar with the settings that they are able to configure, as well as the settings that are non-configurable and that are applied by Microsoft.

Configuring password policies

Password policies determine how often an Office 365 user must change their password. The default Office 365 settings require a user to change their password every 90 days, with a warning being issued 14 days prior to password expiration.

You configure Office 365 password policies using the Office 365 admin center. To perform this action, navigate to the Security & Privacy section under the Settings and click Edit next to Password policy and specify the following options as shown in Figure 3-1:

- **Password never expires** Enabling this setting means that the password does not expire.
- **Days before passwords expire** This is the maximum number of days that a password remains valid. You can set this to values between a minimum of 14 and a maximum of 730 days.
- **Days before the user is notified that their password expires** This determines the number of days before a password expires that the user is sent a notification. This can be set to a value between 1 and 30 days.

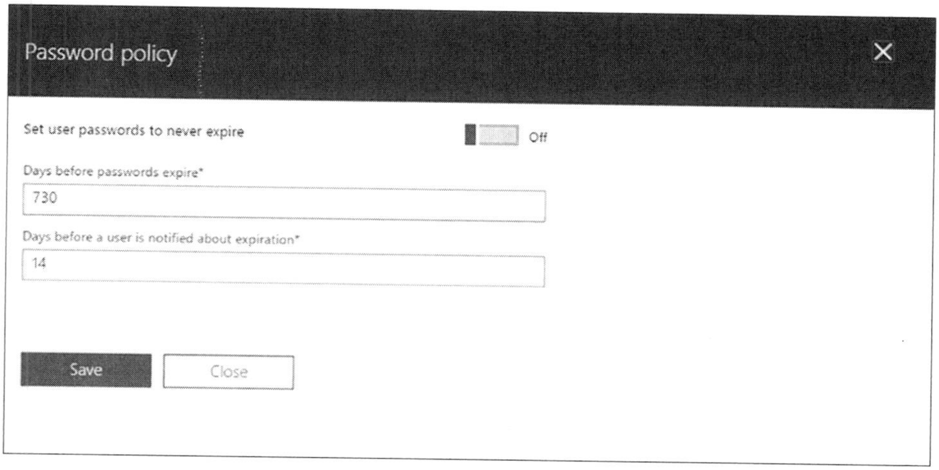

FIGURE 3-1 Default Office 365 password policies

Password expiration duration and password expiration notification settings can be configured using the Set-MsolPasswordPolicy Windows PowerShell cmdlet, which is included in the Azure Active Directory Windows PowerShell module. Whether passwords expire can be set with the Set-MsolUser cmdlet. Use a value of false to ensure that the password will expire, and a value of true to configure the account so that the password will not expire. Using Windows PowerShell to manage cloud identifies is covered in more detail later in the chapter.

Following password complexity policies

Password complexity policies in Office 365 are not able to be configured by administrators and are instead set by Microsoft. The password complexity policies specified by Microsoft require passwords to have the following properties:

- 8 character minimum
- 16 character maximum
- Can include the following characters: A – Z, a – z, 0 – 9 @ # $ % ^ & * - _ + = [ ] { } | \ : ' , . ? / ` ~ " ( ) ;
- Cannot include Unicode characters
- Cannot include spaces
- Cannot contain a dot character '.' Immediately preceding an at '@' symbol

Although you cannot disable Office 365 password complexity requirements using Office 365 Admin Center, you can disable complex password requirements using Windows PowerShell.

Office 365 requires that the last password used cannot be used again. This differs from Active Directory, where a configurable number of recent passwords cannot be reused. This means that a user can rotate their password between a small number of passwords. The lack of a lengthier password history provides a good reason to enable multi-factor authentication on Office 365 user accounts. Multi-factor authentication is covered in more detail later in this chapter.

Office 365 account lockout policies are also managed by Microsoft. If a user performs 10 sequential unsuccessful logon attempts, they will need to respond to a CAPTCHA dialog. This is used to protect Office 365 user accounts from automated password attacks. After an additional 10 sequential unsuccessful logon attempts, the user will be locked out for a time period. This starts at 90 seconds and increases with each subsequent incorrect login attempt. At no point will the account be locked out in such a way that it can only be unlocked by an Office 365 administrator.

> **_MORE INFO_ PASSWORD POLICIES**
>
> You can learn more about Office 365 password policies at the following address: _https://docs.microsoft.com/en-us/azure/active-directory/active-directory-passwords-policy_.

Resetting passwords

Users forgetting their passwords is a staple of the practice of systems administration. Though Microsoft is hinting at moving away from password-based authentication with Windows 10, services such as Office 365 and Azure Active Directory still use passwords as the primary method of authentication.

The drawback of passwords is that the more secure you make them, the less likely users are to remember them. While a password policy that requires a user to change their password every 21 days does marginally increase security, it will also increase the number of calls to the service desk as an increased number of users require administrators to reset their forgotten password. Office 365 provides two basic methods of dealing with forgotten passwords: the first is to have an administrator perform a manual password reset; the second is to allow the user to reset their own password using the self-service password reset mechanism.

Administrator reset

Office 365 administrators can reset user passwords using the Office 365 Admin Center or by using the Set-MsolUserPassword cmdlet, which is part of the Azure Active Directory Windows PowerShell module. You'll learn more about performing operations using the Azure Active Directory Windows PowerShell module later in this chapter.

When you reset a user password using Office 365 Admin Center, Office 365 assigns a new temporary password. This means that the administrator does not choose the temporary password to be assigned. As a way of remembering this temporary password, Office 365 provides you with the option of emailing the password out to one or more email addresses.

Once the password is reset, the reset user password will be displayed on the screen. Because the password is displayed on the screen, an Administrator can perform a reset and use another method to communicate the reset password to the user. For example, you could choose to send an SMS to the user or providing the password verbally using a telephone call. Using an alternative method to communicate the password to the user is more secure than sending the password in clear text using email.

To reset a user password, perform the following steps:

1. In the Office 365 Admin Center, select the Active Users area, which is located under the Users section.

2. In the Active Users area, select the user account for which you need to reset the password. Figure 3-2 shows the Adam Wallen user account selected.

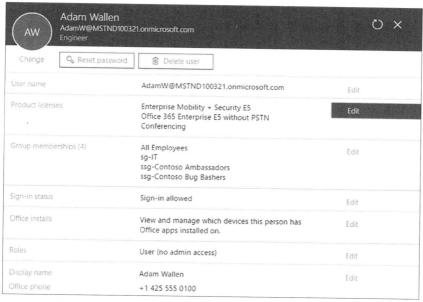

FIGURE 3-2 Select the user in the Active Users area

3. Under the user's name, click Reset Password.

4. Choose between auto-generating a new password or specifying a new password. You can also choose to force the user to change the password when they sign in as shown in Figure 3-3.

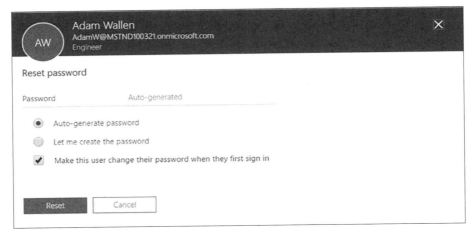

FIGURE 3-3 Reset password

5. Once the password is reset, you can configure the email address to which the new password will be sent as shown in Figure 3-4. Note that if you choose to email the password, that information will be sent in clear text and will not be protected by encryption. Passwords transmitted in clear text over email should always be reset as expeditiously as possible.

FIGURE 3-4 Send reset information in email

6. When you click Reset Password, the temporary password is displayed on the screen. If you haven't chosen to email the password, you should make a note of it here and then forward it to the recipient using another method.

7. Click Finish to complete the password reset operation.

Self-service password reset

Self-service password reset allows users to reset a forgotten password, rather than having to contact an administrator to get them to reset the password.

Self-service password reset has the following prerequisites:

- You must be using an Azure Active Directory tenant. Office 365 functions as an Azure Active Directory tenant, so if you have Office 365, you have met this prerequisite. This Azure Active Directory tenant must be associated with an Azure subscription.

- You must be using Azure Active Directory Premium or Basic. Azure Active Directory comes in Free, Basic, and Premium editions.

- There must be at least one administrator account and one user account in the Azure Active Directory instance.

- The Azure Active Directory Premium or Basic license must be assigned to the administrator and user account.

To configure self-service password reset, perform the following steps:

1. In the Azure portal, open Azure Active Directory and click Password Reset.

2. Select Properties as shown in Figure 3-5. You will see a list of groups for which Self-service Password reset is enabled. By default the SSPRSecurityGroupUsers group has self-service password reset enabled.

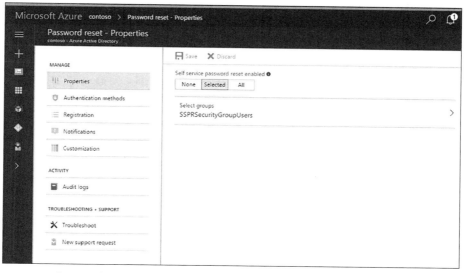

FIGURE 3-5 Password reset properties

3. In the Authentication Methods area, shown in Figure 3-6, you can also require that more than one authentication method be used to perform a password reset. For example, you can require answering a security question and providing a code that is sent via SMS message. The contact settings will be taken from the settings stored with the user's Office 365 / Azure Active Directory user account. You can also provide users with a link to the following webpage, http://aka.ms/ssprsetup, which allows authenticated users to alter their authentication information.

- **Office Phone**   The user's office phone number. This supports the phone call method of verification.

- **Mobile Phone**   The user's mobile number. Supports the phone call and SMS method of verification.

- **Alternate Email Address**   Verification information is sent to a previously specified email address.

- **Security Questions**   Question and answer pairs selected by the user at the authentication information registration page. You can configure which questions are asked through the Azure Management console.

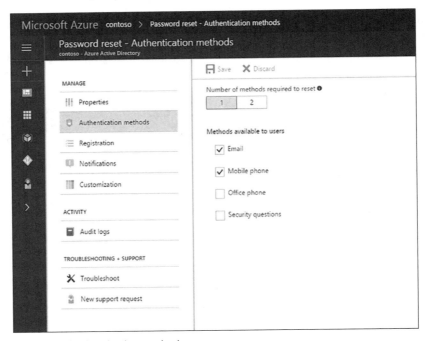

FIGURE 3-6 Authentication methods

Once you have enabled the self-service password reset policy, users will be able to perform self-service password reset by clicking the Can't Access Your Account? link on the Office 365 sign on portal, *portal.microsoftonline.com*.

EXAM TIP

Remember the password complexity requirements and limitations.

Skill 3.2: Manage user and security groups

This skill deals with how you can manage Office 365 user and security groups. You'll also learn about how to bulk import users into Office 365, configure multi-factor authentication, perform a soft delete of a user account, and leverage the Azure Active Directory Graph API for user and group management.

This section covers the following topics:
- Bulk import
- Soft delete
- Multi-factor authentication

Using the bulk import process

The bulk import process allows you to import a list of users from a specially formatted CSV file into Office 365. This CSV file must have the following fields in the first row:
- User Name
- First Name
- Last Name
- Display Name
- Job Title
- Department
- Office Number
- Office Phone
- Mobile Phone
- Fax
- Address

- City
- State or Province
- ZIP or Postal Code
- Country or Region

Each of these fields must be on the first line and each must be separated by a comma ",". Both a sample and a blank CSV file can be downloaded from the Bulk Add Users page.

Once you have populated the CSV file with the account information you want to import, you can complete this operation by performing the following steps:

1. In the Office 365 Admin Center, click On the Active Users node under the Users node.

2. Click More and then click Import multiple users.

3. On the Select a CSV file page, shown in Figure 3-7, select the specially formatted file that has the user account information and click Next.

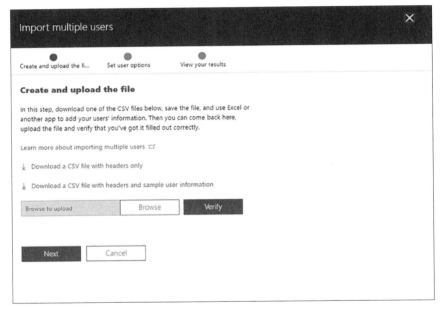

FIGURE 3-7 Select a CSV file

4. On the Import multiple users page, specify whether the users are allowed to sign in and access services. You will also need to specify the user location on this page. You will also need to choose which licenses are assigned as shown in Figure 3-8.

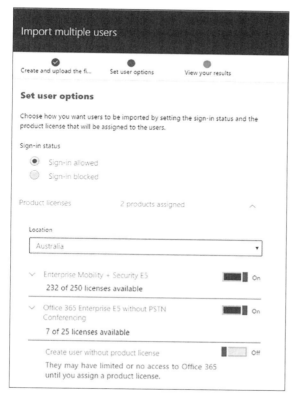

FIGURE 3-8 Import multiple users

5. On the Results page, you will see a list of users created and a list of temporary passwords assigned.

Using soft delete

There are several methods that you can use to delete Office 365 user accounts. Whether the user account is permanently deleted, termed a "hard delete," or is moved to the Azure Active Directory Recycle Bin, termed a "soft delete," depends on the method used to delete the account.

You can use the following methods to delete an Office 365 user account:

Delete the user account from the Office 365 admin portal. This involves navigating to the Users node, selecting the Active Users node, then selecting the user that you want to delete, and selecting Delete User from the list of tasks associated with the user as shown in Figure 3-9.

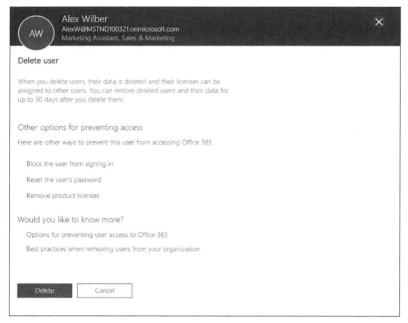

FIGURE 3-9 Delete a user from Office 365 Admin Center

- Deleted using the Remove-MsolUser cmdlet, located in the Azure Active Directory module for Windows PowerShell. More detail on this cmdlet, including how to use it to perform a hard user deletion, rather than just a soft deletion, is covered later in this chapter.

- User accounts can be deleted through the Exchange Admin Center in Exchange Online.

- If directory synchronization is configured, users can be deleted when removed from the on-premises Active Directory Directory Services instance.

You can view a list of soft deleted users in the Deleted Users section, under the Users area of the Office 365 Admin Center. Figure 3-10 shows the deleted Office 365 user account of Alex Wilber. Soft-deleted users remain visible for for 30 days and can be recovered during this period. After this period expires, the user account is deleted and is unrecoverable.

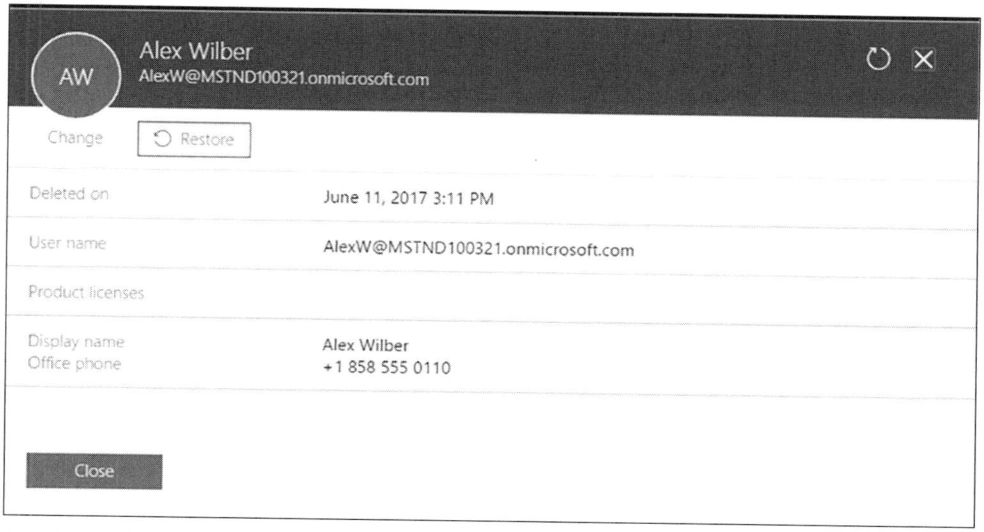

FIGURE 3-10 Deleted user properties

> *MORE INFO* **DELETING USER ACCOUNTS IN OFFICE 365**
>
> You can learn more about deleting Office 365 user accounts at: *https://docs.microsoft.com/en-us/azure/active-directory/active-directory-users-delete-user-azure-portal.*

Enabling multi-factor authentication

When you enable multi-factor authentication for Office 365 users, a user must use two or more forms of authentication before being able to sign on. For example, when signing on, a user might not only have to provide a username and password combination, they might also have to provide a code generated by an application. Multi-factor authentication makes it very difficult for an account to be used by someone other than the owner of that account as it requires not only knowing the password, but having access to the other authentication method.

A username and password remains the primary method of authenticating to Office 365. Office 365 supports the following secondary multi-factor authentication options:

- **Use of a mobile device app** This is an app that can be downloaded from each mobile device vendor's app store. You provide it with QR or numerical code. The app generates a new number every thirty seconds. The user enters this code during sign on.

- **One-time password** This is a single use password that can be used in the event that other secondary multi-factor authentication options are not available. The user can enter this code during sign-on. Once the code is used, the user will need to acquire a new one-time password.

- **A phone call** This involves a phone call to a pre-configured phone number. The user must answer the phone call by entering a code displayed on the screen into the handset.

- **An SMS message** An SMS message containing a code is sent to a pre-configured mobile phone number. The user enters this code when signing on to Office 365.

Enable multi-factor authentication

To enable multi-factor authentication in Office 365, perform the following steps:

1. In the Office 365 Admin Center, navigate to the Users section and click the Active Users section. Click More, and then click Set Up Azure Multi-Factor Authentication.

2. On the Multi-Factor Authentication page, shown in Figure 3-11, select the user for which you want to enable multi-factor authentication, and then click Enable.

FIGURE 3-11 Select users for multi-factor authentication

3. Review the about Enabling Multi-Factor Auth dialog box, shown in Figure 3-12 and then click Enable Multi-Factor Auth.

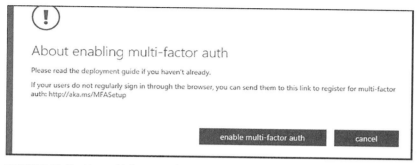

FIGURE 3-12 Enable multi-factor authentication warning

4.   Click close when notified that multi-factor auth has been enabled.

The next time the user signs on, they will be redirected to a webpage that allows them to set up multi-factor authentication. You can also direct the users to navigate to the URL *http://aka.ms/MFASetup*. When they sign in at this URL, they can configure multi-factor authentication.

You can choose between enabling multi-factor authentication, which gives the user the option of using multi-factor authentication, or enforcing multi-factor authentication, which requires the user to use multi-factor authentication. When you enforce multi-factor authentication for a user, you are presented with warning dialog box shown in Figure 3-12. This informs you that the user will need to create app passwords.

Configure app passwords

App passwords allow you to configure application specific passwords for non-browser clients that might not support multi-factor authentication. App specific passwords are enabled by default when you enable multi-factor authentication. App passwords are separate from user passwords, and remain valid even when a user changes their user account password.

You can enable or disable application passwords by performing the following steps:

1.   In the Office 365 Admin Center, select the Active Users node under the Users node and then click Set Up next to Set Multi-Factor Authentication Requirements.

2.   On the Multi-Factor authentication page, click Service Settings.

3.   On the Service Settings page, choose to allow or disallow app passwords. You can also use this page, shown in Figure 3-13, to allow users to suspend multi-factor authentication on a per-device basis by allowing Office 365 to remember the device. You can configure how long the device can be remembered before requiring re-authentication. The default value is 14 days.

FIGURE 3-13 Configure app password settings

Although administrators cannot view or change app passwords, they can force users to recreate app passwords by deleting all existing app passwords. To perform this task, complete the following steps:

1. In the Office 365 Admin Center, select the Active Users node under the Users node and then click Set Up next to Set Multi-Factor Authentication Requirements.

2. On the Multi-Factor authentication page, select the check box next to the user for which you want to delete all existing app passwords and then click Manage User Settings.

3. On the Manage User Settings dialog box, shown in Figure 3-14, select the Delete All Existing App Passwords Generated by The Selected Users and click Save.

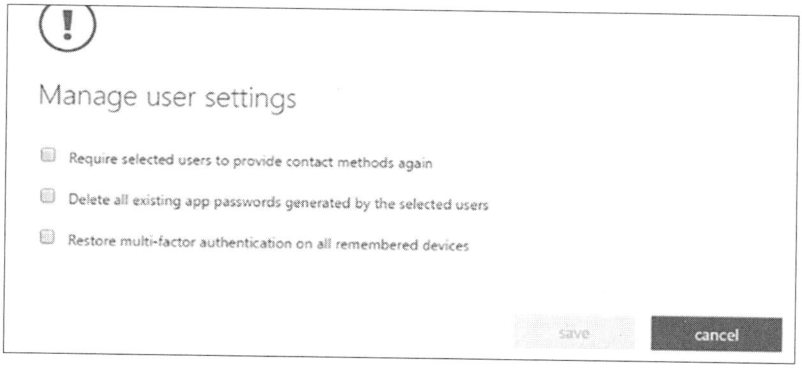

Manage user settings

☐ Require selected users to provide contact methods again

☐ Delete all existing app passwords generated by the selected users

☐ Restore multi-factor authentication on all remembered devices

save   cancel

FIGURE 3-14 Delete existing app passwords

> **MORE INFO** **MULTI-FACTOR AUTHENTICATION**
>
> You can learn more about multi-factor authentication for Office 365 at: *https://support.of-fice.com/en-us/article/Set-up-multi-factor-authentication-for-Office-365-users-8f0454b2-f51a-4d9c-bcde-2c48e41621c6?ui=en-US&rs=en-US&ad=US.*

EXAM TIP

Remember the different multi-factor authentication options that are available for Office 365 user accounts.

Skill 3.3: Manage cloud identities with Windows PowerShell

This skill deals with how you can manage Office 365 user identities using Windows Power-Shell. Although the web-based Administration Center enables you to quickly perform Office 365 user management tasks on individual users, this method is not suited to performing management tasks across a large number of user accounts.

The advantage of using Windows PowerShell is that you can use it to perform user management tasks across some or all of the user accounts stored in Office 365 with one or two lines of code as opposed to manually performing the same set of actions on each user account when using the Office 365 Administration Center.

> **This section covers the following topics:**
> - Configure passwords to never expire
> - Hard delete users
> - Bulk user creation
> - Bulk user license management
> - Bulk update of user properties
> - Additional Azure Active Directory cmdlets

Managing user passwords with Windows PowerShell

If you have the Azure Active Directory Module for Windows PowerShell installed and properly configured, you can use the cmdlets that it contains to manage Office 365 cloud identities. As new features are introduced to Office 365, they often become configurable through Windows PowerShell before the Office 365 Admin Center is updated to allow configuration of these new features.

You can perform the following Office 365 user administration tasks using Windows PowerShell:

- Modify a user's password
- Configure the password policy for the Office 365 tenant (number of days to expire and notification settings)
- Configure whether user passwords expire
- Remove password complexity requirements

You can also use Windows PowerShell to generate a list of users based on their password settings properties, such as being able to generate a list of users who have accounts with passwords configured not to expire or which have accounts which are configured not to require strong passwords.

Changing passwords

You can change a user's password using the Set-MsolUserPassword Windows PowerShell cmdlet. You can also use this cmdlet to force a user to change their password the next time they sign in. So if a user forgets their password and is unable to perform a self-service password reset, you could use the Set-MsolUserPassword Windows PowerShell cmdlet to assign them a new temporary password to access the service which, when they use it to sign on, would immediately require them to create a new password. This new password would need to adhere to the Office 365 password policies.

For example, to change the password of Don Funk to Pa$$w0rd and require him to change it the next time he signs on, issue the following command:

```
Set-MsolUserPassword –UserPrincipalName don.funk@contoso2017er.onmicrosoft.com
–NewPassword Pa$$w0rd –ForceChangePassword $True
```

Configure password expiration

You can use the Set-MsolUser cmdlet from the Azure Active Directory Windows PowerShell module to configure whether an Office 365 user's password expires. This is inadvisable from a security perspective, because a password that is not changed is more likely to be compromised. If you do choose, or are required, to configure an Office 365 user's password to not expire, consider implementing multi-factor authentication as a way of increasing the user account's authentication requirements.

To configure the password of the user Don Funk to never expire, use the command:

```
Set-MsolUser –UserPrincipalName don.funk@contoso2017er.onmicrosoft.com
–PasswordNeverExpires $true
```

You can configure the Office 365 tenancy so that passwords don't expire for any of the user accounts by using the Set-MsolUser cmdlet in conjunction with the Get-MsolUser cmdlet. For example, to configure all user accounts so that their passwords do not expire, use the following command:

```
Get-MsolUser | Set-MsolUser –PasswordNeverExpires $true
```

You can change this back so that the password does expire if it has been configured not to expire by setting the PasswordNeverExpires parameter to $false. For example, to configure Don Funk's user account so that the password follows the existing password policy, use the following command:

```
Set-MsolUser –UserPrincipalName don.funk@contoso2017er.onmicrosoft.com
–PasswordNeverExpires $false
```

You can use a similar technique to the one that you use to configure the Office 365 tenancy so that no user passwords expire to configure the Office 365 tenancy so that all passwords expire according to the tenancy password policy. To do this, issue the following command:

```
Get-MsolUser | Set-MsolUser –PasswordNeverExpires $false
```

Password complexity

Office 365 user accounts stored in Azure Active Directory are subject to the Azure Active Directory password policy. As you saw earlier in this chapter, this means that all user account passwords need to be between 8 and 16 characters long and need to contain three of the following four characteristics: uppercase letters, lowercase letters, numbers, and symbols. You cannot change the Azure Active Directory password policy, because this is set by Microsoft. You cannot use the Office 365 Admin Center to exempt a user account from the Azure Active Directory password policy. You can, however, use a PowerShell command to exempt a user account from the requirement of having a strong password. You can do this with the Set-MsolUser cmdlet and the StrongPasswordRequired parameter. For example, to configure Don Funk's Office 365 user account so that it does not have to conform to the Azure Active Directory password complexity policy, issue the following command:

```
Set-MsolUser -UserPrincipalName don.funk@contoso2017er.onmicrosoft.com
-StrongPasswordRequired $false
```

To switch an account back, pass $True to the parameter instead of $false. For example, to configure Don Funk's Office 365 user account so that it must conform to the Azure Active Directory password complexity policy, issue the following command:

```
Set-MsolUser -UserPrincipalName don.funk@contoso2017er.onmicrosoft.com
-StrongPasswordRequired $true
```

Even though you can exempt a user from the Azure AD password policy using Windows PowerShell and not the Office 365 Admin Center, it would be difficult to find an adequate justification from a security perspective for doing so.

Hard deleting users

As mentioned earlier in this chapter, most user deletion operations move user accounts into the Azure Active Directory Recycle Bin rather than deleting those accounts entirely. Only after the user accounts have been stored in the recycle bin for a period of 30 days are they completely deleted. Once a user has been removed from the Azure Active Directory Recycle Bin, all licenses assigned to that user are reclaimed. Deleting a user so that their account ends up in the recycle bin is sometimes termed "soft deleting."

You can view users that have been soft deleted using the following Windows PowerShell command:

```
Get-MsolUser -ReturnDeletedUsers
```

In some cases, you want to delete a user account entirely, bypassing the Azure Active Directory Recycle Bin. This is called a "hard delete." You can hard delete a specific user as long as you know their UPN. To hard delete the user with the UPN don.funk@adatum346ER. onmicrosoft.com you would issue the following command:

```
Remove-MsolUser -UserPrincipalName don.funk@adatum346ER.onmicrosoft.com -Force
```

If you want to empty all users from the Azure Active Directory Recycle Bin, you can use the following command:

```
Get-MsolUser –ReturnDeletedUsers | Remove-MsolUser –RemoveFromRecycleBin -Force
```

> **MORE INFO** **REMOVE-MSOLUSER**
>
> You can learn more about using Remove-MsolUser at: *https://docs.microsoft.com/en-us/powershell/module/MSOnline/Restore-MsolUser*.

Performing bulk account operations

Earlier in the chapter you learned how to import users stored in a CSV file into Office 365 using the Office 365 Admin Center. You can also perform bulk operations, such as a bulk user import or a bulk change of user properties, using the Azure Active Directory module for Windows PowerShell.

Importing users

You can perform a bulk import of users from a specially formatted CSV file. The CSV file used for bulk import operations requires the fields formatted in the following manner.

```
UserPrincipalName,DisplayName,FirstName,LastName,Password,Department,UsageLocation
```

Once you have the CSV file with all of the user account information that needs to be imported into Office 365, you can use the following command to place the contents of the file NewUsers.csv into the variable $NewUsers:

```
$NewUsers = Import-Csv –path .\NewUsers.csv
```

If you want to license the users during the import process, the next thing need to have account is the SKU ID information. You can store this information in a variable and use with the bulk import command. You place the SKU ID information into a variable by issuing the following command:

```
$Sku = Get-MsolAccountSku
```

Once you have the $Sku variable configured, you enact the following command to import this account information into Office 365:

```
ForEach($NewUser in $NewUsers){New-MsolUser –UserPrincipalName $NewUser.
UserPrincipalName –DisplayName $NewUser.DisplayName –FirstName $NewUser.Firstname –
LastName $NewUser.LastName –Password $NewUser.Password –Department $NewUser.Department
–UsageLocation $NewUser.UsageLocation –LicenseAssignment $Sku.AccountSkuId}
```

You can choose to not include password information. If you do that, Office 365 will assign a random password to each user. The drawback of this is that you will need to make a note of the password, whereas by including it in the CVS file, you can assign a standard first password to all users and then use a second command to require them to change their password to a new and unique one on next sign on.

Bulk licensing users

In the previous example, you saw how to bulk import users, assigning them licenses at the same time. You can also choose not to license the users at the time of import and instead perform a bulk license operation. If you are going to use this method, you must ensure that the Usage Location property of the user account is already set. You cannot perform this operation if this property has not been configured.

You can bulk license users by generating a CSV file that has a single header titled UPN and which contains a list of users by UPN, one UPN per line.

To import this list into a variable, use the Import-Csv cmdlet in the following manner:

```
$LicenseUsers = Import-Csv =Path .\LicenseUsers.csv
```

The next step is to get the appropriate SKU and to place this into a second Windows PowerShell variable. You do this by issuing the following command:

```
$Sku=Get-MsolAccountSku
```

Once this is done, you can apply the license information by issuing the following command:

```
ForEach($LicenseUser in $LicenseUsers){Set-MsolUserLicense –UserPrincipalName
$LicenseUser.UPN –AddLicenses $Sku.AccountSkuId}
```

Bulk update user properties

You can perform a bulk update of user properties using a combination of the Get-MsolUser and the Set-MsolUser cmdlets. Depending on how you want to update the properties, you can pipe the results of the Get-MsolUser cmdlet straight into the Set-MsolUser cmdlet. As an alternative, you can also read the output of the Get-MsolUser cmdlet into a variable, and then use a ForEach loop to update the user properties using the Set-MsolUser cmdlet.

For example, to update the city property of each user in the HR department to Melbourne, issue the command:

```
Get-MsolUser –Department "HR" | Set-MsolUser –City "Melbourne"
```

Using Azure Active Directory cmdlets

When loaded, the Azure Active Directory module for Windows PowerShell allows you to manage an Office 365 tenancy as well as the Azure Active Directory instance that supports this tenancy. For organizations that have just implemented a simple Office 365 deployment, only some of these cmdlets will be relevant. For organizations that want to take greater advantage of the integration between Office 365 and Azure Active Directory, understanding of what cmdlets are available and what they can accomplish is important.

The Azure Active Directory cmdlets can be separated into the following categories:

- User management
- Group and role management
- Service principal management
- Domain management
- Single sign on management
- Subscription and license management
- Company information and service management
- Administrative unit management

User management cmdlets

There are nine cmdlets in the Azure Active Directory Windows PowerShell module that can be used to manage Office 365 and Azure Active Directory user accounts. Several of these cmdlets were already been covered earlier in this chapter, but are included here for the same of completeness and to assist with exam revision.

- **Convert-MsolFederatedUser** This cmdlet allows you to update a user in a domain that originally used single sign-on/identity federation authentication, but which has been converted to standard authentication. When using this cmdlet, it is necessary to provide a new password for the user.
- **Get-MsolUser** This cmdlet allows you to retrieve user information or information about a number of users.
- **New-MsolUser** This cmdlet allows you to create a new Office 365 or Azure Active Directory user. To grant the user access to Office 365 services, they must be assigned a license.

- **Remove-MsolUser**   Use this cmdlet when you want to remove an Office 365 or Azure Active Directory user. This cmdlet allows you to remove the user, associated licenses and data.

- **Restore-MsolUser**   You can use this cmdlet to restore a user who is in the Azure Active Directory recycle bin. Deleted user accounts are only stored in the Azure Active Directory Recycle Bin for 30 days.

- **Set-MsolUser**   Use this cmdlet when you want to modify the properties of an existing Office 365 or Azure Active Directory user. You do not use this cmdlet is to set licenses, passwords, or user principal names as separate cmdlets exist for these tasks.

- **Set-MsolUserPassword**   Use this cmdlet to change a user password. You can only use this cmdlet for Office 365 and Azure Active Directory users with standard identities. You cannot use this cmdlet to change the password of users from domains that use single sign on or identity federation.

- **Set-MsolUserPrincipalName**   You use this cmdlet to alter the User Principal Name of a user. You can use this cmdlet to move a user between a domain that uses standard identities and a domain that uses single sign on/identity federation.

- **Redo-MsolProvisionUser**   You use this cmdlet if you need to re-attempt provisioning of an Office 365 or Azure Active Directory user in the event that a prior attempt to create the user object generated a validation error.

Group and role management cmdlets

The Azure Active Directory module for Windows PowerShell includes a number of cmdlets that you can use to manage roles and groups. These include the following:

- **Add-MsolGroupMember**   Use this cmdlet to add members to an Office 365 or Azure Active Directory security group. You can add user accounts to security groups or have one security group as a member of another security group.

- **Add-MsolRoleMember**   Use this cmdlet to add users to an Office 365 or Azure Active Directory role.

- **Get-MsolGroup**   You use this cmdlet to get group information from Office 365 or Azure Active Directory.

- **Get-MsolGroupMember**   You use this cmdlet to get membership information for an Office 365 or Azure Active Directory group.

- **Get-MsolRole**   Use this cmdlet to get a list of administrator roles for Office 365 or Azure Active Directory.

- **Get-MsolRoleMember**   Use this cmdlet to determine membership information for a specific role.

- **Get-MsolUserRole**   You use this cmdlet to determine to which administrator roles a specific Office 365 or Azure Active Directory user belongs.

- **New-MsolGroup**   You use this cmdlet to add a new security group to Office 365 or Azure Active Directory.
- **Redo-MsolProvisionGroup**   You use this cmdlet to re-attempt the provisioning of a group if you previously received a validation error when attempting this task.
- **Remove-MsolGroup**   You can use this cmdlet to delete a security group from Office 365 or Azure Active Directory.
- **Remove-MsolGroupMember**   You use this cmdlet when you want to remove a user or security group account from an existing Office 365 or Azure Active Directory security group.
- **Remove-MsolRoleMember**   Use this cmdlet to remove a user account from an existing administrator role.
- **Set-MsolGroup**   Use this cmdlet to modify the properties of an existing security group.

Service principal management cmdlets

The Azure Active Directory module for Windows PowerShell includes a number of cmdlets that you can use to manage the configuration of service principals in Azure Active Directory. These cmdlets include:

- **Set-MsolServicePrincipal**   Use this cmdlet to update an Azure Active Directory service principal. For example, you can use it to update the display name, configure the service principal name, enable, or disable the service principal.
- **New-MsolServicePrincipal**   Use this cmdlet to create a new service principal. You would do this when you need a representation of "service principal" objects in Azure Active Directory of a Line Of Business (LOB) Application or an on-premises server like Exchange, SharePoint, or Lync.
- **Get-MsolServicePrincipal**   Use this cmdlet to retrieve a list of service principals stored in Azure Active Directory, or information about a specific service principal.
- **New-MsolServicePrincipalAddress**   You can use this cmdlet to create a new service principal address object. You can then use this new object when updating the address of a service principal.
- **Get-MsolServicePrincipalCredential**   You use this cmdlet to view a list of credentials that are tied to a specific service principal.
- **New-MsolServicePrincipalCredential**   You use this cmdlet to add new credentials to a service principal. You can also use this cmdlet to add credential keys for an application.
- **Remove-MsolServicePrincipalCredential**   Use this cmdlet when you want to remove a credential key from a specific service principal.

Domain management cmdlets

The Azure Active Directory module for Windows PowerShell includes a number of cmdlets that you can use to manage domains stored within Azure Active Directory. These cmdlets include the following:

- **Confirm-MsolDomain** You use this cmdlet to confirm that you own a specific domain. You do this by adding a special TXT DNS record to the domain. Use his cmdlet after first adding the domain to Azure Active Directory with the New-MsolDomain cmdlet.
- **Get-MsolDomain** Use this cmdlet to retrieve company domains.
- **Get-MsolDomainVerificationDns** You use this cmdlet to determine which DNS records you need to configure to confirm a domain.
- **New-MsolDomain** You use this cmdlet to create a new domain that uses managed identities. Although you can use this cmdlet to create a domain that uses federated identities, Microsoft recommends using the New-MsolFederatedDomain cmdlet for this task.
- **Remove-MsolDomain** Use this cmdlet to remove a domain from Azure Active Directory. You can only remove a domain if it has no users or groups with email addresses stored.
- **Set-MsolDomain** Use this cmdlet to update settings for a domain.
- **Set-MsolDomainAuthentication** Use this cmdlet to alter the authentication model for the Azure Active Directory domain between single-sign on / federated and standard. This cmdlet updates Azure Active Directory settings. Microsoft recommends using the Convert-MsolDomainToStandard or Convert-MsolDomainToFederated cmdlets when performing a domain conversion operation.
- **Get-MsolPasswordPolicy** Use this cmdlet when you want to view the current password policy.
- **Set-MsolPasswordPolicy** Use this cmdlet when you want to change the current password policy.

Single sign-on management cmdlets

The Azure Active Directory module for Windows PowerShell includes a number of cmdlets related to managing federated, also known as single sign-on domains.

- **New-MsolFederatedDomain** Use this cmdlet to add a new identity federated/single sign-on domain and to configure the relying party trust settings between Azure Active Directory and the on premises Active Directory Federation Services server.
- **Convert-MsolDomainToStandard** Use this cmdlet to convert an Azure Active Directory domain between identity federation/single sign-on to standard authentication. This will remove relying party trust settings between the on-premises Active Directory Federation Services 2.0 server and Azure Active Directory. Once the conversion is

complete, all existing users will have their authentication switched from single sign-on to standard authentication. When this process occurs, each converted user is assigned a temporary password. These passwords are stored in a file that is accessible to an administrator who can then forward them to users allowing them to sign in to Office 365.

- **Convert-MsolDomainToFederated** You use this cmdlet if you want to convert an Azure Active Directory domain from standard authentication to identity federation/ single sign-on. Performing this action also includes configuring the relying party trust settings between Azure Active Directory and the on-premises Active Directory Federation Services 2.0 server.

- **Get-MsolFederationProperty** Use this cmdlet to get key settings from Azure Active Directory and the on-premises Active Directory Federation Services 2.0 server.

- **Get-MsolDomainFederationSettings** You use this cmdlet to get key settings from Azure Active Directory.

- **Remove-MsolFederatedDomain** Use this cmdlet when you want to remove a specific identity federated/single sign-on domain from Azure Active Directory. Executing this cmdlet also removes relying party trust settings from the on-premises Active Directory Federation Services 2.0 server.

- **Set-MsolDomainFederationSettings** You use this cmdlet to update the settings of an identity federated/single sign-on domain.

- **Set-MsolADFSContext** You use this cmdlet to configure the credentials that connect the on-premises Active Directory Federation Services 2.0 server and Azure Active Directory.

- **Update-MsolFederatedDomain** You use this cmdlet to alter settings in both Azure Active Directory and Active Directory Federation Services. You would use this cmdlet if you needed to update the URLs or certificate information, such as when you need to renew certificates.

Subscription and license management cmdlets

The Azure Active Directory module for Windows PowerShell includes a number of cmdlets related to subscription and license management. These cmdlets allow you to view and manage organizational subscription information, as well as allow you to manage the licenses assigned to Office 365 users. Cmdlets in this category include the following:

- **Get-MsolSubscription** You can use this cmdlet to view all of the subscriptions that your organization has purchased.

- **Get-MsolAccountSku** You can use this cmdlet to generate a list of all SKUs that your organization owns.

- **New-MsolLicenseOptions** This cmdlet allows you to create a new License Options object.

- **Set-MsolUserLicense** Use this cmdlet to adjust the licenses assigned to a user. You can use this cmdlet to assign a new license, remove a license, or update a license.

Company information and service management cmdlets

The Azure Active Directory module for Windows PowerShell includes a number of cmdlets you can use to manage company and service information. You can use the following cmdlets for this task:

- **Add-MsolForeignGroupToRole** You use this cmdlet when you want to add a partner tenant security group to an Office 365 or Azure Active Directory role.

- **Connect-MsolService** You use this cmdlet to initiate a connection to Azure Active Directory. You use this cmdlet in a command at the start of each Windows PowerShell session when you want to manage Office 365 or Windows Azure Active Directory.

- **Get-MsolCompanyInformation** Use this cmdlet to retrieve company-level information from Azure Active Directory.

- **Get-MsolContact** You use this cmdlet when you want to get information about a specific contact object, or to generate a list of contacts.

- **Get-MsolPartnerContract** This cmdlet is used by partner organizations to generate a list of partner specific contracts.

- **Get-MsolPartnerInformation** This cmdlet is used by partner organizations to generate partner-specific information.

- **Redo-MsolProvisionContact** You use this cmdlet if you have attempted to provision a contact object and have received a validation error.

- **Remove-MsolContact** You use this cmdlet when you want to delete an object from Azure Active Directory.

- **Set-MsolCompanyContactInformation** You use this cmdlet when you want to configure company level contact-preferences, such as email addresses for billing, marketing, and technical notifications.

- **Set-MsolCompanySecurityComplianceContactInformation** You use this cmdlet when you want to configure company level contact preferences for security and compliance correspondence.

- **Set-MsolCompanySettings** Use this cmdlet to modify company-level configuration settings.

- **Set-MsolDirSyncEnabled** Use this cmdlet to enable or disable directory synchronization.

- **Set-MsolPartnerInformation** This cmdlet is used by partners to configure partner-specific settings. These settings are visible by all tenants to which the partner has access.

Administrative unit management cmdlets

The Azure Active Directory module for Windows PowerShell includes a number of cmdlets that you can use to manage administrative units. These include the following cmdlets:

- **Add-MsolAdministrativeUnitMember** Use this cmdlet to add an account to an administrative unit.
- **Add-MsolScopedRoleMember** You use this cmdlet to add an account to a specific role that is scoped to a specific administrative unit.
- **Get-MsolAdministrativeUnit** You use this cmdlet to generate a list of administrative units stored in Azure Active Directory.
- **Get-MsolAdministrativeUnitMember** You use this cmdlet to get a list of all of the members of a specific administrative unit.
- **Get-MsolScopedRoleMember** You use this cmdlet to get a membership list of a specific role that is scoped to a specific administrative unit.
- **New-MsolAdministrativeUnit** Use this cmdlet when you want to add a new administrative unit to Azure Active Directory.
- **Remove-MsolAdministrativeUnit** You use this cmdlet to remove an administrative unit from Azure Active Directory.
- **Remove-MsolAdministrativeUnitMember** You use this cmdlet to remove a user account from a specific administrative unit.
- **Remove-MsolScopedRoleMember** You use this cmdlet to remove a user account from a specific role that is scoped to a specific administrative unit.
- **Set-MsolAdministrativeUnit** You use this cmdlet to modify the properties of an administrative unit stored in Azure active directory.

> *MORE INFO* **AZURE ACTIVE DIRECTORY MANAGEMENT**
>
> You can learn more about using PowerShell to manage Azure Active Directory at:
> *https://docs.microsoft.com/en-us/powershell/module/MSOnline/?view=azureadps-1.0.*

EXAM TIP

Remember each of the different PowerShell cmdlets and how you can use them to manage different aspects of Office 365 tenant users and groups.

Thought experiment

In this thought experiment, apply what you've learned about this objective. You can find the answers to these questions in the "Answers" section at the end of this chapter.

You are in the process of configuring the user password reset policy for Office 365 users at Adatum. All users at Adatum have all been issued mobile phones and they do not have traditional landlines. Each user at Adatum has only a single email account. Company policy requires that email accounts hosted by third-party providers not be used for Adatum-related business or activities. Within these constraints, you want to configure the strongest user password reset policy possible.

As a security measure, you intend to require multi-factor authentication for all users that are authenticating to the organization's Office 365 deployment. You have the following objectives:

1. You want to ensure that users always use multi-factor authentication when connecting to Office 365.

2. You only want to allow applications that support multi-factor authentication to be able to connect to your organization's Office 365 deployment. Users should not be able to configure a special password for each app.

In addition, you need to add 1,000 user new user accounts to Office 365. These user accounts are stored in an appropriately formatted CSV file. Additionally, all users that are in the Sydney office are being moved to the Melbourne office. As there are 500 users, you would rather use Windows PowerShell to perform a bulk user account property update.

Finally, one of the users that you need to deal with on a regular basis, Don Funk, uses the UPN don.funk@adatum.com.

With this information in mind, answer the following questions:

1. Which password reset options should you enable for Adatum?

2. How many authentication methods should be required in the user password reset policy?

3. How should you configure multi-factor authentication for all Adatum users??

4. How should you configure app passwords?

5. You delete a user using the Office 365 Admin Center. How many days does a user's account remain in the Azure Active Directory Recycle Bin before it is permanently deleted?

6. You have a file containing the details of users which you wish to bulk import into Office 365. Which format must a file use if you are going to use the Office 365 Admin Center to perform this operation?

7. Which cmdlets would you use to bulk import user accounts from the CSV file using Windows PowerShell?

8. Which cmdlets would you use to bulk update the properties of existing Office 365 user accounts?

9. You want to configure Don Funk's Office 365 user account so that his password does not expire. The password expiration settings of other accounts in the Office 365 tenancy should not change. With the Azure Active Directory PowerShell Module loaded, which PowerShell command would you use to accomplish this goal?

10. Several user accounts in your organization's Office 365 tenancy have been configured so that the passwords do not expire. You want to reconfigure all accounts so that their passwords expire in line with the password policy configured for the Office 365 tenancy. With the Azure Active Directory PowerShell Module installed, which of the following commands would you use to accomplish this goal?

11. Don Funk has called the service desk. He has forgotten his password and needs someone in the IT department to reset it for him. You decide to reset the password to the temporary password "Pa$$w0rd", but also want to require Don to change his password the next time he signs on. When the Azure Active Directory Windows PowerShell module is loaded, which of the following cmdlets could you use to accomplish this goal?

12. You need to allow Don Funk to use a 7 character password. The Azure Active Directory password policy does not allow 7 character passwords. Which of the following Windows PowerShell commands would you use to exempt Don Funk's Office 365 user account from the Azure Active Directory password policy?

13. Which cmdlet must you use each time you use a Windows PowerShell session to manage an Office 365 tenancy?

Thought experiment answers

This section contains the solution to the thought experiment. Each answer explains why the answer choice is correct.

1. As users at Adatum have no traditional landlines and Adatum related business should not be sent to external email accounts, the remaining password reset options are Mobile Phone and Security Question.

2. As you want to configure the strongest user password reset policy and you only have two available methods, requiring both the Mobile Phone and the Security Question provides you with the strongest possible option.

3. You should enforce multi-factor authentication for all Office 365 users. This will mean that they must use multi-factor authentication rather than it being optional.

4. You should disable app passwords so that they cannot be used.

5. User accounts remain in the Azure Active Directory Recycle Bin for 30 days before they are permanently deleted.

6. The file containing user account information must be in CSV format for you to be able to use it to import user accounts into Office 365 using the Office 365 admin center.

7. You use the Import-CSV cmdlet, ForEach and the New-MSOLUser cmdlets to bulk import usre accounts from a specially formatted CSV file.

8. You would use the Get-MsolUser cmdlet to retrieve a list of all users in the Sydney office and the Set-MsolUser cmdlet to update their office information so that it was set to the Melbourne office.

9. Set-MsolUser -UserPrincipalName don.funk@adatum.com -PasswordNeverEpires $true.

10. Get-MsolUser | Set-MsolUser -PasswordNeverExpires $false.

11. Set-MsolUserPassword -UserPrincipalName don.funk@adatum.com -NewPassword Pa$$w0rd -ForceChangePassword $True.

12. Set-MsolUser -UserPrincipalName don.funk@adatum.com -StrongPasswordRequired $False.

13. Connect-MsolService.

Chapter summary

- Administrators can configure how long before a password must be changed and the number of days warning before a change is required.

- Office 365 password complexity policies are not configurable by tenant administrators.

- Passwords must be between 8 and 16 characters, must have a mix of three of uppercase, lowercase, numbers and symbols, and cannot include a dot character preceding an @ symbol.

- Administrators can reset passwords or can configure self-service password reset.

- Self-service password reset options include office phone, mobile phone, alternate email address, and security questions.

- You can use the Office 365 Admin Center to bulk import users from a specially formatted CSV file.

- When you delete a user from Office 365, their account remains in the Azure Active Directory Recycle Bin for 30 days. The account can be recovered during this period.

- Multi-factor authentication can be configured to allow or require users to use a second form of authentication, including office telephone, mobile phone, alternate email address, or answering a series of questions.

- Use the Set-MsolUser cmdlet with the –PasswordNeverExpires parameter to configure users password to never expire.

- Use the Remove-MsolUser cmdlet with the –Force parameter to hard delete users
- Use the Import-CSV cmdlet to import users in a properly formatted spreadsheet into a variable, and then use a foreach command with the New-MsolUser cmdlet to import these users into Office 365 / Azure Active Directory.
- Use the Set-MsolUser cmdlet with the –AddLicenses parameter to perform bulk licensing operations.
- Use Get-MsolUser cmdlet with the Set-MsolUser cmdlet to bulk update user properties.

CHAPTER 4

Implement and manage identities by using Azure AD Connect

A substantial number of organizations integrate their on-premises Active Directory Domain Services deployment with the Azure Active Directory instance that supports their Office 365 tenancy. Unlike a cloud-only deployment, where all of the user, group, and contact accounts are stored and managed in Azure Active Directory, integration allows users, groups, and contacts created on-premises to synchronize up to Office 365. Integration can occur through synchronization, which is the subject of this chapter, or through federation, the subject of Chapter 5, "Implement and manage federated identities."

Skills in this chapter

- Skill 4.1: Prepare on-premises Active Directory for Azure AD Connect
- Skill 4.2: Setup Azure AD Connect tool
- Skill 4.3: Manage Active Directory users and groups with Azure AD Connect in place

Skill 4.1: Prepare on-premises Active Directory for Azure AD Connect

This skill deals with preparing your on-premises Active Directory environment for synchronization of user accounts, group accounts, and mail-enabled contacts to the Azure Active Directory instance that supports the Office 365 tenancy. To master this skill, you'll need to understand the different Active Directory synchronization tools, the steps needed to prepare an on-premises Active Directory instance for Azure AD Connect, what to do if your on-premises Active Directory uses a non-routable domain name, what to think about when it comes to planning filtering of user account objects for synchronization, and what to do if you have a multiple forest environment.

This section covers the following topics:

- Active Directory synchronization tools
- Cleaning up existing Active Directory objects
- UPN suffixes and non-routable domain names
- Plan for filtering Active Directory
- Support for multiple forests

Azure Active Directory Connect

Azure Active Directory Connect is Microsoft's replacement for DirSync and Azure Active Directory Sync tools. Azure AD Connect is designed to streamline the process of configuring connections between on-premises deployment. Rather than perform some of the complex tasks outlined in this chapter and the next, the Azure Active Directory Connect tool is designed to make the process of configuring synchronization between an on-premises Active Directory deployment and Azure Active Directory as frictionless as possible.

Azure Active Directory Connect can automatically configure and install simple password synchronization or Federation / Single Sign-on, depending on your organizational needs. When you choose the Federation with AD FS option, Active Directory Federation Services is installed and configured, as well as a Web Application Proxy server to facilitate communication between the on-premises AD FS deployment and Microsoft Azure Active Directory.

The Azure Active Directory Connect tool supports the following optional features, as shown in Figure 4-1:

- **Exchange hybrid deployment** This option is suitable for organizations that have an Office 365 deployment where there are mailboxes hosted both on-premises and in the cloud.

- **Exchange mail public folders** This feature allows organizations to synchronize mail-enabled public folder objects from an on-premises Active Directory environment to Office 365.

- **Azure AD app and attribute filtering** Selecting this option gives you the ability to be more selective about which attributes are synchronized between the on-premises environment and Azure AD.

- **Password synchronization** Synchronizes a hash of the user's on-premises password Azure AD. When the user authenticates to Azure AD, the submitted password is hashed using the same process and if the hashes match, the user is authenticated. Each time the user updates their password on-premises, the updated password hash synchronizes to Azure AD.

- **Password writeback** Password writeback allows users to change their passwords in the cloud and have the changed password written back to the on-premises Active Directory instance.

- **Group writeback**   Changes made to groups in Azure AD are written back to the on-premises AD instance.
- **Device writeback**   Information about devices registered by the user in Azure AD is written back to the on-premises AD instance.
- **Directory extension attribute sync**   Allows you to extend Azure AD schema based on extensions made to your organization's on-premises Active Directory instance.

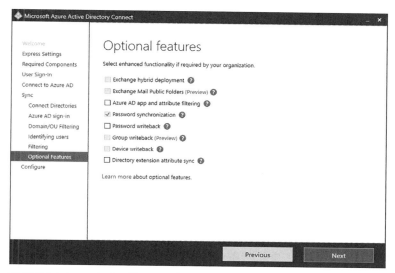

FIGURE 4-1 Azure Active Directory Connect optional features

> **MORE INFO** **AZURE ACTIVE DIRECTORY CONNECT**
>
> You can learn more about Azure Active Directory Connect at *https://docs.microsoft.com/en-us/azure/active-directory/connect/active-directory-aadconnect*.

Cleaning up existing Active Directory objects

Before you deploy Azure AD Connect, it is prudent to ensure that your on-premises Active Directory environment is healthy. You should also have an excellent understanding of the current state of the Active Directory environment. This should include performing an audit to determine the following:

- Do any Active Directory objects use invalid characters?
- Do any Active Directory objects have incorrect Universal Principal Names (UPNs)?
- What are the current domain and forest functional levels?
- Are any schema extensions or custom attributes in use?

Prior to deploying Azure AD Connect, you should ensure that you have performed the following tasks:

- Remove any duplicate proxyAddress attributes
- Remove any duplicate userPrincipalName attributes
- Ensure that blank or invalid userPrincipalName attribute settings have been altered so that the setting contains only a valid UPN
- Ensure that for user accounts that the cn and samAccountName attributes have been assigned values
- Ensure that for group accounts, the member, alias, and displayName (for groups with a valid mail or proxyAddress attribute) are populated
- Ensure that the following attributes do not contain invalid characters:
  - givenName
  - sn
  - samAccountName
  - givenName
  - displayName
  - mail
  - proxyAddress
  - mailNickName

UPNs that are used with Office 365 can only contain the following characters:

- Letters
- Numbers
- Periods
- Dashes
- Underscores

Rather than having to perform this operation manually, Microsoft provides some tools that allow you to automatically remediate problems that might exist with attributes prior to deploying Azure AD Connect.

IdFix

The IdFix tool, which you can download from Microsoft's website, allows you to scan an Active Directory instance to determine if any user accounts, group accounts, or contacts have problems that will cause them not to synchronize between the on-premises instance of Active Directory and the Office 365 instance of Azure Active Directory. IdFix can also perform repairs on objects that would otherwise be unable to sync. IdFix runs with the security context of the currently signed on user. This means that if you want to use IdFix to repair objects in the forest that have problems, the security account you use to run IdFix must have permissions to modify those objects. The IdFix tool is shown in Figure 4-2 displaying an account detected with an incorrectly configured userPrincipalName.

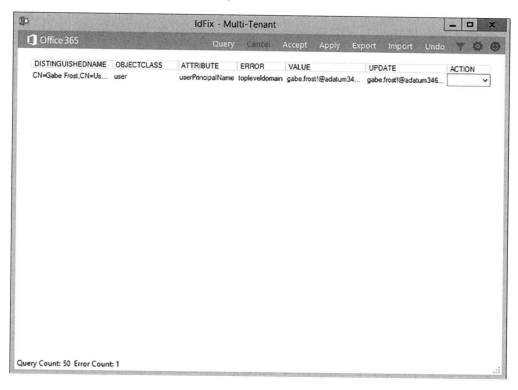

FIGURE 4-2 IdFix finds user with a problematic UPN.

> **MORE INFO IDFIX**
>
> You can download IdFix at the following address *http://www.microsoft.com/en-us/down-load/details.aspx?id=36832*.

ADModify.NET

ADmodify.NET is a tool that allows you to make changes to specific attributes for multiple objects. If you are using ADSIEdit or the Advanced mode of the Active Directory Users and Computers console, you are only able to modify the attribute of one object at a time. For example, Figure 4-3 shows ADModify.NET used to modify the format of the userPrincipalName attribute for a number of user accounts so that it conforms to a specific format.

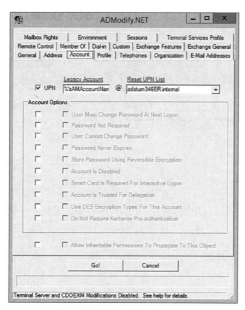

FIGURE 4-3 ADModify.NET

You can also use ADModify.NET to perform other systems administration tasks, such as configuring a large number of accounts, so that the users have to change their password at next logon or to disable multiple accounts.

> **MORE INFO ADMODIFY.NET**
>
> You can learn more about ADModify.NET at *https://technet.microsoft.com/en-us/library/aa996216(v=EXCHG.65).aspx*.

Using UPN suffixes and non-routable domains

Prior to performing synchronization between an on-premises Active Directory environment and an Azure Active Directory instance used to support an Office 365 tenancy, you must ensure that all user account objects in the on-premises Active Directory environment are configured with a value for the UPN suffix that is able to function for both the on-premises environment and Office 365.

This is not a problem when an organization's internal Active Directory domain suffix is a publicly routable domain. For example, a domain name, such as contoso.com or adatum.com that is resolvable by public DNS servers will suffice. Things become more complicated when the organization's internal active directory domain suffix is not publicly routable. For example, Figure 4-4 shows the adatum346ER.internal non-routable domain.

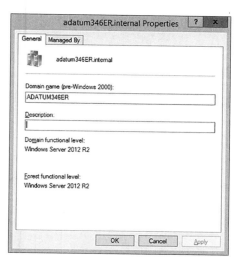

FIGURE 4-4 Non routable domain

If a domain is non-routable, the default routing domain—for example, adatum346ER. onmicrosoft.com—should be used for the Office 365 UPN suffix. This requires modifying the UPN suffix of accounts stored in the on-premises Active Directory instance. Modification of UPN after initial synchronization has occurred is not supported. This means that you need to ensure that on-premises Active Directory UPNs are properly configured prior to performing initial synchronization using Azure AD Connect.

To add a UPN suffix to the on-premises Active Directory in the event that the Active Directory domain uses a non-routable namespace, perform the following steps:

1. Open the Active Directory Domains And Trust console and select Active Directory Domains And Trusts.

2. On the Action menu, click Properties.

3. On the UPN Suffixes tab, enter the UPN suffix to be used with Office 365. Figure 4-5 shows the UPN suffix of adatum346ER.onmicrosoft.com.

FIGURE 4-5 Non routable domain

4. Once the UPN suffix has been added in Active Directory Domains And Trusts, you can assign the UPN suffix to user accounts. You can do this manually as shown in Figure 4-6 by using the Account tab of the user's properties dialog box in Active Directory Users And Computers.

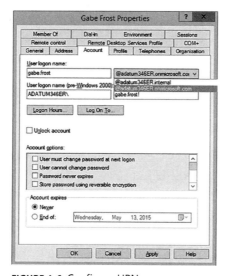

FIGURE 4-6 Configure UPN

5. You can use tools like ADModify.NET to reset the UPNs of multiple accounts as shown in Figure 4-7.

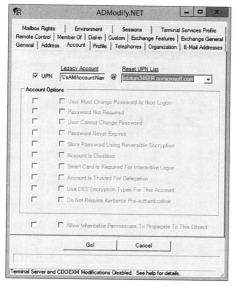

FIGURE 4-7 ADModify.NET

6. You can also use Microsoft PowerShell scripts to reset the UPNs of multiple user accounts. For example, the following script resets UPN suffixes of all user accounts in the adatum346ER.internal domain to adatum346ER.onmicrosoft.com.

```
Get-ADUser -Filter {UserPrincipalName -like "*@adatum346ER.internal"} -SearchBase
"DC=adatum346ER,DC=internal" |
ForEach-Object {
$UPN =
$_.UserPrincipalName.Replace("adatum346.internal","adatum346ER.onmicrosoft.com")
Set-ADUser $_ -UserPrincipalName $UPN
}
```

Planning for filtering Active Directory

When you use Azure AD Connect to synchronize on-premises Active Directory to an Azure Active Directory instance, the default setting is to have all user accounts, group accounts, and mail-enabled contact objects synchronized up to the cloud. For some organizations, synchronizing everything is exactly what they want. Other organizations want to be more selective about which objects are synchronized from the on-premises Active Directory environment to the Azure Active Directory instance that supports the Office 365 tenancy.

With Azure AD Connect, you can choose to filter based on the following options as shown in Figure 4-8:

- **Domain based** In a forest with multiple domains, you can configure filtering so that only objects from some domains, and not others, are filtered.

- **Organizational unit (OU) based**   With this filtering type, you choose which objects are filtered based on their location within specific organizational units.

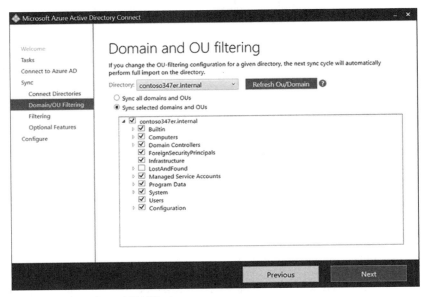

FIGURE 4-8 Domain and OU filtering

You can also configure filtering on the basis of group membership, as shown in Figure 4-9. You can configure separate group based filters for each forest or domain synchronized using Azure AD Connect.

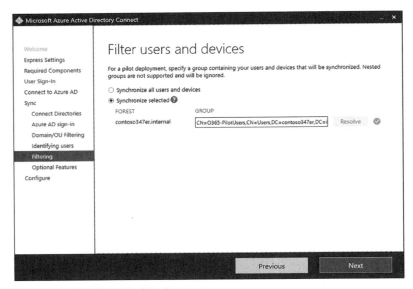

FIGURE 4-9 Filter Users And Devices

While Azure AD Connect will address most organization's synchronization requirements, the most comprehensive tool that you can use to filter synchronization is the Synchronization Rules Editor, shown in Figure 4-10. You can use this tool to modify existing synchronization rules, but also to create new rules. Rather than configuring synchronization on a per-domain or per-OU basis, you can tailor rules for individual objects and specific Active Directory attributes.

FIGURE 4-10 Synchronization Rules Editor

Supporting multiple forests

The Azure Active Directory Connect tool also supports synchronization from multiple on-premises Active Directory forests to a single Azure Active Directory instance. Multiple forest synchronization to a single Azure AD instance is supported only when a single Azure AD Connect server is in use. Microsoft does not support multiple Azure AD Connect servers synchronizing with a single Azure AD instance, whether there is one or multiple forests being synchronized.

By default, Azure AD Connect will assume that:

- A user has a single enabled account. Also, the forest where this account is located must host the directory that is used to authenticate the user. This assumption is used in both password sync and federation scenarios. On the basis of this assumption, the UserPrincipalName and sourceAnchor/immutableID are drawn from this forest.

- Each user has a single mailbox, and the forest that host that mailbox is the best source of attributes visible in the Exchange Global Address List (GAL). In the event that a user doesn't have an associated mailbox, any configured forest can function as the source for these attribute values.

- If a user account has a linked mailbox, there will be an account in an alternate forest used for the sign-in process.

- The key to synchronizing user accounts from multiple forests is that only one user account from all synchronized forests should represent the user. This means that the synchronization engine should have a way to determine when accounts in separate forests represent the same user. You can configure how the Azure AD Connect sync engine identifies users on the Uniquely Identifying Your Users page, shown in Figure 4-11 using one of the following options:

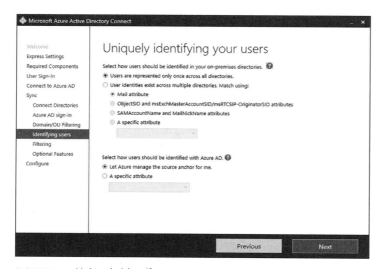

FIGURE 4-11 Uniquely identify users

- Match users using the mail attribute
- Match user using ObjectSID and msExchangeMasterAccountSID/msRTCIP-Orgiginator-SID attributes
- Match user using SAMAccountName and MailNickName attributes
- Specify a custom attribute upon which to match names

> **MORE INFO MULTI-FOREST SYNCHRONIZATION**
>
> You can learn more about multi-forest synchronization at the following address: *https://docs.microsoft.com/en-us/azure/active-directory/connect/active-directory-aadconnect-topologies*.

Azure AD Connect Sign-on options

Azure AD Connect supports a variety of sign in options. You configure which one you want to use when setting up Azure AD Connect as shown in Figure 4-12. The default method, Password Synchronization, is appropriate for the majority of organizations who will use Azure AD Connect to synchronize identities to the cloud.

FIGURE 4-12 User sign-in

Password synchronization

Hashes of on-premises Active Directory user passwords synchronize to Azure AD and changed password synchronize to Azure AD immediately. Actual passwords are never sent to Azure AD and are not stored in Azure AD. Allows for single sign-on for users of computers that are joined to an Active Directory domain that synchronizes to Azure AD. Password synchronization also allows you to enable password write-back for self-service password reset functionality through Azure AD.

Pass-through authentication

When authenticating to Azure AD, the user's password is validated against an on-premises Active Directory domain controller. Passwords and password hashes are not present in Azure AD. Pass-through authentication allows for on-premises password policies to apply. Pass-though authentication requires that Azure AD Connect have an agent on a computer joined to the domain that hosts the Active Directory instance that contains the relevant user accounts. Pass-through authentication also allows single sign-on for users of domain joined machines.

With pass-through authentication, the user's password is validated against the on-premises Active Directory controller. The password doesn't need to be present in Azure AD in any form. This allows for on-premises policies, such as sign-in hour restrictions, to be evaluated during authentication to cloud services.

Pass-through authentication uses a simple agent on a Windows Server 2012 R2 domain-joined machine in the on-premises environment. This agent listens for password validation requests. It doesn't require any inbound ports to be open to the Internet.

In addition, you can also enable single sign-on for users on domain-joined machines that are on the corporate network. With single sign-on, enabled users only need to enter a username to help them securely access cloud resources.

Active Directory Federation

This allows users to authenticate to Azure AD resources using on-premises credentials. It also requires the deployment of an Active Directory Federation Services infrastructure. You will learn more about this in Chapter 5, "Implement and manage federated identities for single sign on."

> **MORE INFO** **SIGN-IN OPTIONS**
>
> You can learn more about sign-in options, consult the following article: *https://docs.microsoft.com/en-us/azure/active-directory/connect/active-directory-aadconnect-user-signin.*

Skill 4.2: Set up Azure AD Connect

This skill deals with the process of deploying Azure AD Connect as well as configuring initial Azure AD Connect options. To master this skill, you'll need to understand how the on-premises Active Directory environment needs to be configured to support Azure AD Connect, the hardware and software specifications of the computer that hosts Azure AD Connect, and the privileges required by the account that is used to configure Azure AD Connect. You'll also need to understand soft match filtering, be able to identify synchronized attributes, and also know how to configure password synchronization.

This section covers the following topics:

- Azure AD Connect installation requirements
- Installing Azure AD Connect
- Filtering
- Identify synchronized attributes
- Password sync

Meeting the Azure AD Connect installation requirements

Prior to installing Azure AD Connect, you should ensure that your environment, Azure AD Connect computer, and account used to configure Azure AD Connect meets the software, hardware, and privilege requirements. This means that you need to ensure that your Active Directory environment is configured at the appropriate level, that the computer on which you will run Azure AD Connect has the appropriate software and hardware configuration, and that the account that you use to install Azure AD Connect has been added to the appropriate security groups.

> **MORE INFO** **AZURE AD CONNECT PREREQUISITES**
>
> You can learn more about Azure AD Connect prerequisites at the following address: https://docs.microsoft.com/en-us/azure/active-directory/connect/active-directory-aadcon-nect-prerequisites.

Azure AD and Office 365 requirements

Before you can install and configure Azure AD Connect, you need to ensure that you have configured an additional domain for Office 365. You learned about configuring additional domains in Chapter 1, "Provision Office 365." By default, an Azure AD tenant will allow 50,000 objects, though when you add and verify an additional domain, this limit increases to 300,000 objects. If you require more than 300,000 objects in your Azure AD instance, you can open a support ticket with Microsoft. If you require more than 500,000 objects in your Azure AD instance, you'll need to acquire an Azure AD Premium or Enterprise Mobility and Security license.

On-premises Active Directory environment requirements

Azure AD Connect requires that the on-premises Active Directory environment be configured at the Windows Server 2003 forest functional level or higher. Forest functional level is dependent on the minimum domain functional level of any domain in a forest. For example, if you have five domains in a forest, with four of them running at the Windows Server 2012 R2 domain functional level and one of them running at the Windows Server 2003 domain functional level, then Windows Server 2003 will be the maximum forest functional level. As

Windows Server 2003 is no longer supported by Microsoft without a custom support agreement, your organization should have domain controllers running Windows Server 2008 at least. Microsoft security best practice is to have domain controllers deployed with Microsoft's most recent version of the server operating system, so in theory you should have domain controllers running Windows Server 2016. To support the Azure AD Connect password write-back functionality, you'll either need domain controllers running Windows Server 2008 R2 or Windows Server 2008 with all service packs applied as well as hotfix KB2386717.

You can check the forest functional level using the Active Directory Domains and Trusts console. To do this, perform the following steps:

1. Open the Active Directory Domains and Trusts console.

2. Select the Active Directory Domains and Trusts node.

3. On the Actions menu, click Raise Forest Functional Level.

4. The dialog box displays the current functional level and, if possible, provides you with the option of upgrading the forest functional level. Figure 4-13 shows the forest functional level configured at Windows Server 2012 R2, which is the highest possible forest functional level for an organization where all domain controllers are running the Windows Server 2012 R2 operating system. If all the domain controllers are running the Windows Server 2016 operating system, it would be possible to raise the domain and forest functional level to Windows Server 2016.

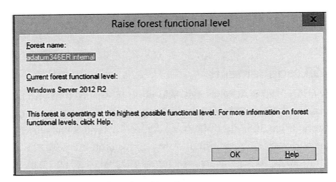

FIGURE 4-13 Forest functional level

You can also check the forest functional level by using the following Microsoft PowerShell command:

```
(Get-ADForest).ForestMode
```

Azure AD Connect Server requirements

Azure AD Connect is software that you install on a computer that manages the process of synchronizing objects between the on-premises Active Directory and the Azure Active Directory instance that supports the Office 365 tenancy. You can install Azure AD Connect on computers running the following operating systems:

- Windows Server 2008 (x86 and x64)
- Windows Server 2008 R2 (x64)
- Windows Server 2012 (x64)
- Windows Server 2012 R2 (x64)
- Windows Server 2016

Azure AD Connect cannot be installed on Windows Server 2003. As Windows Server 2003 is no longer supported by Microsoft, and you are a diligent administrator, you will of course not have Windows Server 2003, or Windows XP for that matter, in your environment.

Azure AD Connect has the following requirements:

- Must be installed on a Windows Server instance that has the GUI version of the operating system installed. You cannot install Azure AD connect on a computer running the Server Core operating system.

- You can deploy Azure AD Connect on a computer that is either a domain controller, a member server or, if you use the custom options, a stand alone server.

- If installing on versions of Windows Server prior to Windows Server 2012, ensure that all service packs, updates, and relevant hotfixes are applied. As a diligent administrator, you have already done this so it isn't necessary to remind you of this.

- If you want to use the password synchronization functionality, you need to ensure that Azure AD connect is deployed on Windows Server 2008 R2 SP1 or later.

- The server hosting Azure AD Connect requires .NET Framework 4.5.1 or later.

- The server hosting Azure AD Connect requires Microsoft PowerShell 3.0 or later.

- The server hosting Azure AD Connect must not have PowerShell Transcription enabled through group policy.

- If you ware deploying Azure AD Connect with Active Directory Federation Services, you must use Windows Server 2012 R2 or later for the Web Application Proxy and Windows remote management must be enabled on the servers that will host AD FS roles.

- If global administrators will have multi factor authentication enabled (MFA), then the URL *https://secure.aadcdn.microsoftonline-p.com* must be configured as a trusted site.

Connectivity Requirements

The computer with Azure AD Connect installed must be a member of a domain in the forest that you want to synchronize, and must have connectivity to a writable domain controller in each domain of the forest you wish to synchronize on the following ports:

- DNS: TCP/UDP Port 53
- Kerberos: TCP/UDP Port 88
- RPC: TCP Port 135
- LDAP: TCP/UDP Port 389
- SSL: TCP Port 443
- SMB: TCP 445

The computer with Azure AD Connect installed must be able to establish communication with the Microsoft Azure servers on the Internet over TCP port 443. The computer with Azure AD Connect installed can be located on an internal network as long as it can initiate communication on TCP port 443. The computer hosting Azure AD Connect does not need a publicly routable IP address. The computer hosting Azure AD Connect always initiates synchronization communication to Microsoft Azure. Microsoft Azure Active Directory does not initiate synchronization communication to the computer hosting Azure AD Connect on the on-premises network.

While you can install Azure AD Connect on a domain controller, Microsoft recommends that you deploy Azure AD Connect on computer that does not host the domain controller role. If you are going to be replicating more than 50,000 objects, Microsoft recommends that you deploy SQL Server on a computer that is separate from the computer that will host Azure AD Connect. If you plan to host the SQL Server instance on a separate computer, ensure that communication is possible between the computer hosting Azure AD Connect and the computer hosting the SQL Instance on TCP port 1433.

If you are going to use a separate SQL Server instance, you must perform installation of Azure AD Connect using the command line. A GUI install of Azure AD Connect always deploys an instance of SQL Server Express. If you are using a full SQL Server instance, ensure that the account used to install and configure Azure AD Connect has "systems administrator" rights on the SQL instance and that the service account used for Azure AD Connect has "public" permissions on the Azure AD Connect database.

Hardware requirements

The hardware requirements of the computer that hosts Azure AD Connect depend on the number of objects in the Active Directory environment that you need to sync. The greater the number of objects that you need to sync, the steeper the hardware requirements. Table 4-X provides a guide to the requirements, with all configurations requiring at least a 1.6 GHz processor.

TABLE 4-2 Azure AD Connect computer hardware requirements

Number of objects in Active Directory	Memory	Storage
Fewer than 10,000	4 GB	70 GB
10,000–50,000	4 GB	70 GB
50,000–100,000	16 GB	100 GB
100,000–300,000	32 GB	300 GB
300,000–600,000	32 GB	450 GB
More than 600,000	32 GB	500 GB

It's important to note that during the planning phase a new Office 365 tenancy has a limit of 50,000 objects. However, once the first domain is verified, this limit is increased to 300,000 objects. Organizations that need to store more than 300,000 objects in an Azure Active Directory instance that supports an Office 365 tenancy should contact Microsoft Support.

SQL Server requirements

When you deploy Azure AD connect, you have the option of having Azure AD Connect install a SQL Server Express instance, or you can choose to have Azure AD Connect leverage a full instance of SQL Server. SQL Server Express is limited to a maximum database size of 10 GB. In terms of Azure AD Connect, this means that Azure AD Connect is only able to manage 100,000 objects. This is likely to be adequate for all but the largest environments.

For environments that require Azure AD Connect to manage more than 100,000 objects, you'll need to have Azure AD Connect leverage a full instance of SQL Server. Azure AD Connect can use all versions of Microsoft SQL Server, from Microsoft SQL Server 2008 with the most recent service pack through to SQL Server 2016 SP1. It is important to note that SQL Azure is not supported as a database for Azure AD Connect. If deploying a full instance of SQL Server to support Azure AD Connect, ensure that the following prerequisites are met:

- **Use a case-insensitive SQL collation** Case insensitive collations have the _CI_ identifier included in their name. Case sensitive collations (those that use the _CS_ designation) are not supported for use with Azure AD Connect.

- **You can only use one sync engine per SQL instance** If you have an additional Azure AD Connect sync engine, or if youare using Microsoft Identity Manager in your environment, each sync engine requires its own separate SQL instance.

Installation account requirements

The accounts that you use to install and configure Azure AD Connect have the following requirements:

- The account used to configure Office 365 must have the Administrator permission in the Office 365 tenant. If you create a service account in Office 365 to use in place of the account with tenant administrator permissions, ensure to configure the account with a password that does not expire.

- The account used to install and configure Azure AD Connect must have Enterprise Administrator permissions within the on-premises Active Directory forest if you will be using express installation settings. This account is only required during installation and configuration. Once Azure AD Connect is installed and configured, this account no longer needs Enterprise Administrator permissions. Best practice is to create a separate account for Azure AD Connect installation and configuration and to temporarily add this account to the Enterprise Admins group during the installation and configuration process. Once Azure AD Connect is installed and configured, this account can be removed from the Enterprise Admins group. You should not attempt to change the account used after Azure AD Connect is setup and configured, since Azure AD Connect always attempts to run using the original account.

- The account used to install and configure Azure AD Connect must be a member of the local Administrators group on the computer on which Azure AD Connect is installed.

Installing Azure AD Connect

Installing Azure AD Connect with express settings is appropriate if your organization has a single Active Directory forest and you wish to use password synchronization for authentication. The Azure AD Connect express settings are appropriate for most organizations. To obtain Azure AD connect, download it from the following website: *http://go.microsoft.com/ fwlink/?LinkId=615771.*

To install Azure AD Connect with Express settings, perform the following steps:

1. Double click on the AzureADConnect.msi file that you've downloaded from the Microsoft download center and click Run on the security warning shown in Figure 4-14.

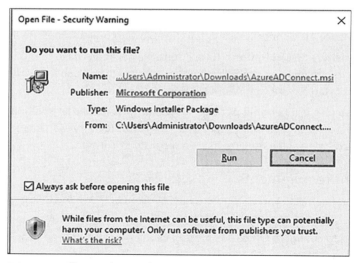

FIGURE 4-14 file security warning

2. Azure AD Connect will be installed on your computer. When the installation is complete, you will be presented with the splash screen. You must agree to the license terms and privacy notice as shown in Figure 4-15 and then click Continue.

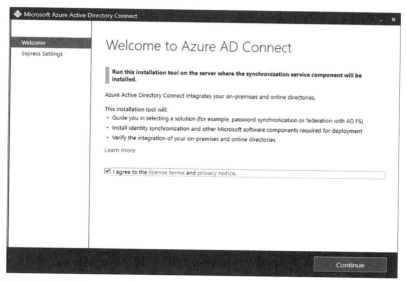

FIGURE 4-15 Welcome to Azure AD Connect

3. If your organization has an internal non-routable domain it will be necessary for you to use custom settings. Figure 4-16 shows the non-routable domain contoso2017er. internal in use. To use custom settings, click Customize.

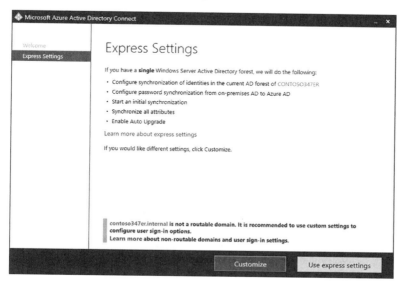

FIGURE 4-16 Express settings

4. On the Install Required Components page, shown in Figure 4-17, choose between the following options:

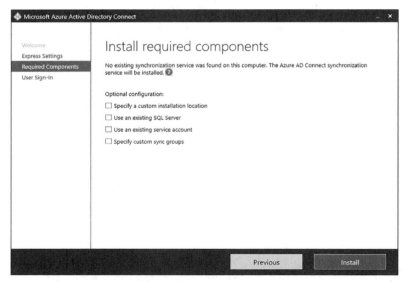

FIGURE 4-17 Install Required Components

- **Specify a custom installation location**   Choose this option if you want to install Azure AD Connect in a separate location, such as on another volume.
- **Specify an existing SQL Server**   Choose this option if you want to specify an alternate SQL server instance. By default, Azure AD Connect will install a SQL Server Express instance.
- **Use an existing service account**   You can configure Azure AD Connect to use an existing service account. By default, Azure AD Connect will create a service account. You can configure Azure AD Connect to use a Group Managed Service account if you are installing Azure AD Connect on a computer running Windows Server 2012 or later. You'll need to use an existing service account if you are using Azure AD Connect with a remote SQL Server instance or if communication with Azure will occur through a proxy server that requires authentication.
- **Specify custom sync groups**   When you deploy Azure AD Connect, it will create four local groups on the server that hosts the Azure AD Connect Instance. These groups are the Administrators group, Operators group, Password Reset group, and the Browse group. If you want to use your own set of groups, you can specify them here. These groups must be local to the host server and not a member of the domain.

5. Once you have specified which custom options you require, and you can select none if you want, but you have to perform a custom installation because you have a non-routable domain on-premises, click Install.

6. On the User sign-in page, shown in Figure 4-18, specify what type of sign on you want to allow. You can choose between the following options, the details of which were covered earlier in this chapter, with most organizations choosing password synchronization as this is the most straightforward:

- Password Synchronization

- Pass-through authentication

- Federation with AD FS

- Do not configure

- Enable single sign-on

FIGURE 4-18 User sign-in options

7. On the Connect To Azure AD page, provide the credentials of a global admin account. Microsoft recommends you use an account in the default onmicrosoft.com domain associated with the Azure AD instance you will be connecting to. If you choose the Federation with AD FS option, ensure that you do not sign in using an account in a domain that you will enable for federation. Figure 4-19 shows sign-in with a password synchronization scenario.

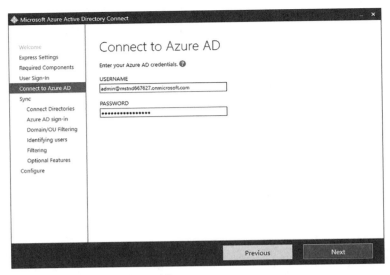

FIGURE 4-19 Connect to Azure AD

8. Once Azure AD Connect has connected to Azure AD, you will be able to specify the directory type to synchronize as well as the forest. Click Add Directory to add a specify forest. When you add a forest by clicking Add Directory, you will need to specify the credentials of an account that will perform periodic synchronization. Unless you are certain that you have applied the minimum necessary privileges to an account, you should provide Enterprise Administrator credentials and allow Azure AD Connect to create the account as shown in Figure 4-20. This will ensure that the account is only assigned the privileges necessary to perform synchronization tasks.

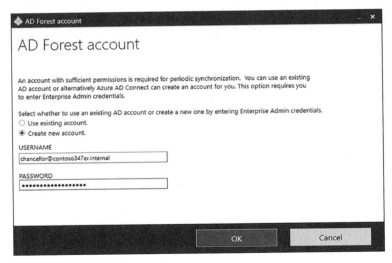

FIGURE 4-20 AD Forest Account

9. Once the credentials have been verified, as shown in Figure 4-21, click Next.

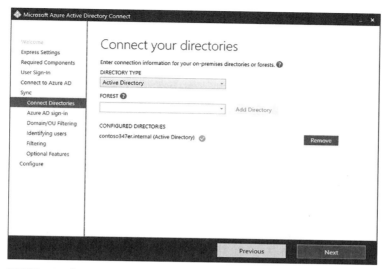

FIGURE 4-21 Connect Your Directories

10. On the Azure AD Sign-In configuration page, shown in Figure 4-22, review the UPN suffix and then inspect the on-premises attribute to use as the Azure AD username. You'll need to ensure that accounts use a routable Azure AD username. You learned about configuring UPN suffixes earlier in the chapter.

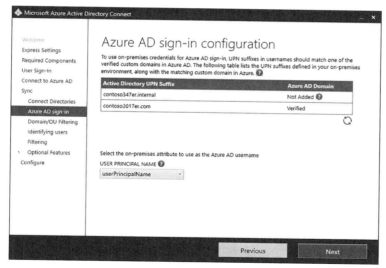

FIGURE 4-22 Azure AD Sign-In Configuration

11. On the Domain And OU Filtering page, shown in Figure 4-23, select whether you want to sync all objects, or just objects in specific domains and OUs.

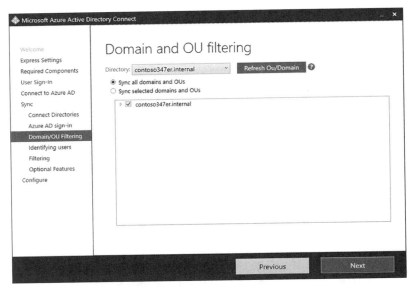

FIGURE 4-23 Domain And OU Filtering

12. On the Uniquely Identifying Users page, shown in Figure 4-24, specify how users are to be identified. By default users should only have one representation across all directories. In the event that users exist in multiple directories, you can have matches identified by a specific active directory attribute, with the default being the mail attribute.

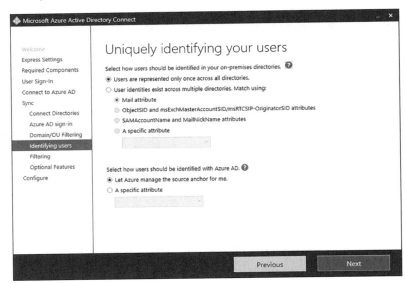

FIGURE 4-24 Uniquely Identifying Users

13. On the Filter Users And Devices page, specify whether you want to synchronize all users and devices, or only members of a specific group. Figure 4-25 shows members of the O365-PilotUsers group being configured so that their accounts will be synchronized with Azure.

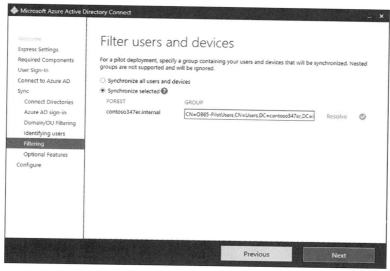

FIGURE 4-25 Filter Users And Devices

14. On the Optional Features page, shown in Figure 4-26, select any optional features that you want to configure. These features include:

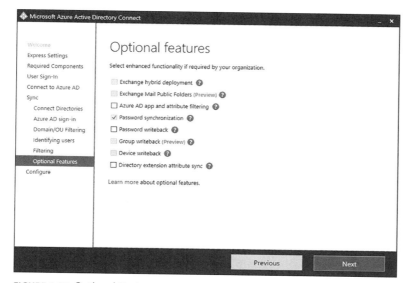

FIGURE 4-26 Optional Features

- Exchange hybrid deployment
- Exchange Mail Public Folders
- Azure AD app and attribute filtering
- Password synchronization
- Password writeback
- Group writeback
- Device writeback
- Directory extension attribute sync

15. On the Ready To Configure page, shown in Figure 4-27, you can choose to start synchronization or to enable staging mode, where synchronization will prepare to be run, but will not synchronize any data with Azure AD.

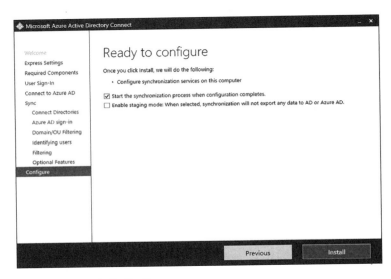

FIGURE 4-27 Ready To Configure

MORE INFO **AZURE AD CONNECT CUSTOM INSTALLATION**

To install Azure AD Connect with the custom settings, consult the following article: *https://docs.microsoft.com/en-us/azure/active-directory/connect/active-directory-aadconnect-get-started-custom.*

Identifying synchronized attributes

Azure AD Connect synchronizes some, but not all, attributes from the on-premises Active Directory instance to Azure Active Directory instance that supports an Office 365 tenancy. 143 separate attributes synchronize, depending on whether the object is a user account, a group account, or a mail enabled contact object. These attributes are as listed in Table 4-3.

TABLE 4-3 List of attributes synchronized by Azure AD Connect

accountEnabled	MsExchArchiveGUID	msExchTeamMailboxOwners
Assistant	MsExchArchiveName	msExchTeamMailboxShare PointLinkedBy
altRecipient	msExchArchiveStatus	msExchTeamMailboxSharePointUrl
authoring	msExchAssistantName	msExchUCVoiceMailSettings
C	msExchAuditAdmin	msExchUsageLocation
Cn	msExchAuditDelegate	msExchUserHoldPolicies
Co	msExchAuditDelegateAdmin	msOrg-IsOrganizational
company	msExchAuditOwner	msRTCSIP-ApplicationOptions
countryCode	MsExchBlockedSendersHash	msRTCSIP-DeploymentLocator
department	msExchBypassAudit	msRTCSIP-Line
description	MsExchBypassModerationFrom DLMembersLink	msRTCSIP-OwnerUrn
displayName	MsExchBypassModerationLink	msRTCSIP-PrimaryUserAddress
dLMemRejectPerms	msExchCoManagedByLink	msRTCSIP-UserEnabled
dLMemSubmitPerms	msExchDelegateListLink	msRTCSIP-OptionFlags
ExtensionAttribute1	msExchELCExpirySuspensionEnd	objectGUID
ExtensionAttribute10	msExchELCExpirySuspensionStart	oOFReplyToOriginator
ExtensionAttribute11	msExchELCMailboxFlags	otherFacsimileTelephone
ExtensionAttribute12	MsExchEnableModeration	otherHomePhone
ExtensionAttribute13	msExchExtensionCustomAttribute1	otherIpPhone
ExtensionAttribute14	msExchExtensionCustomAttribute2	otherMobile
ExtensionAttribute15	msExchExtensionCustomAttribute3	otherPager
ExtensionAttribute2	msExchExtensionCustomAttribute4	otherTelephone
ExtensionAttribute3	msExchExtensionCustomAttribute5	pager

ExtensionAttribute4	MsExchGroupDepartRestriction	photo
ExtensionAttribute5	MsExchGroupJoinRestriction	physicalDeliveryOfficeName
ExtensionAttribute6	msExchHideFromAddressLists	postalCode
ExtensionAttribute7	MsExchImmutableID	postOfficeBox
ExtensionAttribute8	msExchLitigationHoldDate	PreferredLanguage
ExtensionAttribute9	msExchLitigationHoldOwner	proxyAddresses
Facsimiletelephonenumber	MsExchMailboxGuid	PublicDelegates
givenName	msExchMailboxAuditEnable	pwdLastSet
GroupType	msExchMailboxAuditLogAgeLimit	reportToOriginator
hideDLMembership	MsExchModeratedByLink	ReportToOwner
homephone	MsExchModerationFlags	samAccountName
Info	MsExchRecipientDisplayType	sn
Initials	msExchRecipientTypeDetails	St
ipPhone	MsExchRemoteRecipientType	streetAddress
L	msExchRequireAuthToSendTo	targetAddress
legacyExchangeDN	MsExchResourceCapacity	TelephoneAssistant
Mail	MsExchResourceDisplay	telephoneNumber
mailnickname	MsExchResourceMetaData	thumbnailphoto
managedBy	MsExchResourceSearchProperties	title
Manager	msExchRetentionComment	unauthOrig
Member	msExchRetentionURL	url
middleName	MsExchSafeRecipientsHash	userAccountControl
Mobile	MsExchSafeSendersHash	userCertificate
msDS-HABSeniorityIndex	MsExchSenderHintTranslations	UserPrincipalName
msDS-PhoneticDisplayName	msExchTeamMailboxExpiration	userSMIMECertificate

Syncing Passwords

Password Sync allows the synchronization of user account passwords from on-premises Active Directory to the Azure Active Directory instance that supports the Office 365 tenancy. The advantage of this is that users can sign on to Office 365 using the same password that they use to sign in to computers on the on-premises environment. Password Sync does not provide single sign-on or federation. This topic is covered in more detail by Chapter 5, "Implement and manage federated identities."

When you enable Password Sync, the on-premises password complexity policies override password complexity policies configured for the Azure Active Directory instance that supports the Office 365 tenancy. This means that any password that is valid for an on-premises user will be valid within Office 365 even if it would not be normally.

Password expiration works in the following way: the password of the account of the cloud user object is set to never expire. Each time the user account password is changed in the on-premises Active Directory instance, which change replicates to the Azure Active Directory instance that supports the Office 365 tenancy. This means that it is possible for a user account's password to expire on the on-premises Active Directory instance, but that user can still use the same password to sign on to Office 365. The next time they sign on to the on-premises environment, they are forced to change their password and that change replicates up to the Azure Active Directory instance that supports the Office 365 tenancy.

When Password Sync is enabled and you disable a user's account in the on-premises Active Directory instance, the user's account in the Azure Active Directory instance that supports the Office 365 tenancy is disabled within a few minutes. If Password Sync is not enabled and you disable user account in the on-premises Active Directory instance, then the user's account in the Azure Active Directory instance that supports the Office 365 tenancy is not disabled until the next full synchronization.

Skill 4.3: Manage Active Directory users and groups with Azure AD Connect in place

This skill deals with managing Active Directory users and groups once you have configured Azure AD Connect. To master this skill you'll need to understand the concept of source of authority and that in most cases, you'll need to continue to manage users and groups using your on-premises Active Directory tools and then wait for, or force, synchronization to make those changes become apparent within Office 365.

> **This section covers the following topics:**
> - Create users and groups
> - Modify users and groups
> - Delete users and groups
> - Schedule synchronization
> - Force synchronization

Create users and groups

Source of authority is a very important concept when it comes to creating users and groups in an environment where Azure AD Connect is configured to synchronize an on-premises Active Directory with the Azure Active Directory instance that supports the Office 365 tenancy. When you create a user or group in the on-premises Active Directory instance, the on-premises Active Directory instance retains authority over that object. Objects created within the on-premises Active Directory instance that are within the filtering scope of objects synchronized via Azure AD Connect will replicate to the Azure Active Directory instance that supports the Office 365 tenancy.

Newly created on-premises user and group objects will only be present within the Azure Active Directory instance that supports the Office 365 tenancy after synchronization has occurred. You can force synchronization to occur using the Synchronization Service Manager tool.

It's important to remember that user accounts created in Office 365 by the synchronization process will not automatically be assigned Office 365 licenses. This means when you are creating new user accounts in the on-premises environment after you've initially configured

Azure AD Connect, you'll also need to use Office 365 Admin Center, or PowerShell, to provision those accounts with Office 365 licenses.

One of the simplest methods to assign licenses to a large number of accounts is by using PowerShell. To accomplish this task using Microsoft PowerShell, you need to first ensure that a usage location is set for each unlicensed user, and then to assign a license using the proper SKU identifier.

To determine which Office 365 users have not been properly configured with a license, enact the following Microsoft PowerShell command:

```
Get-MsolUser -UnlicensedUsersOnly
```

To assign all unlicensed users to a specific location, use the following command, where <location> is the location to which you wish to assign the unlicensed users:

```
Get-MsolUser -UnlicensedUsersOnly | Set-MsolUser -UsageLocation <location>
```

You'll need to apply the account SKU ID to each account. The way you can do this is first by assigning SKU information to a variable with the following command:

```
$Sku=Get-MsolAccountSku
```

Once you have this information, you can use the following command to apply the appropriate account SKU ID to correctly license each account.

```
Get-MsolUser -UnlicensedUsersOnly | Set-MsolUser -AddLicenses $Sku.AccountSkuID
```

Modifying users and groups

Source of authority is again important when it comes to making modifications to users and groups. Remember that modifications that occur in the on-premises Active Directory overwrite the current state of the objects within the Azure Active Directory instance that supports the Office 365 tenancy. The only exception to this rule is with the assignment of licenses, which only occurs using the Office 365 Admin Center or Microsoft PowerShell tools.

Modifications made to on-premises user and group objects will only be present within the Azure Active Directory instance that supports the Office 365 tenancy after synchronization has occurred. By default, synchronization occurs every three hours. You can force synchronization to occur using the Synchronization Service Manager tool or by using Microsoft PowerShell.

Deleting users and groups

With deletion, the concept of source of authority again is very important. When you want to delete a user or group account that created in the on-premises Active Directory instance, you should use tools, such as Active Directory Users and Computers, or Active Directory Administrative Center, to remove that user. When you delete the user or group using this method, the user will be deleted from the on-premises Active Directory instance and then, when synchronization occurs, will be deleted from the Azure Active Directory instance that supports the Office 365 tenancy.

When you delete a user from Office 365, their account remains in the Azure Active Directory Recycle Bin for 30 days. This means that you can recover the account online should it be necessary to do so. If you delete a user from your on-premises Active Directory environment, but have enabled the on-premises Active Directory Recycle Bin, recovering the user from the on-premises Active Directory Recycle Bin will recover the user account in Office 365. If you don't have Active Directory Recycle Bin enabled, you will need to create another account with a new GUID.

In some cases synchronization doesn't work properly and objects that are deleted from the on-premises Active Directory instance don't delete from the Azure Active Directory instance that supports the Office 365 tenancy. In this circumstance you can use the Remove-MsolUser, Remove-MsolGroup, or Remove-MsolContact Microsoft PowerShell cmdlets to manually remove the orphaned object.

> **MORE INFO** **REMOVING OBJECTS THAT WON'T DELETE**
>
> You can learn more about removing objects created through synchronization that won't delete from Office 365 at: *https://support.microsoft.com/en-us/kb/2619062*.

Managing synchronization

You can manage synchronization using a variety of tools, including PowerShell cmdlets that are part of the ADSync PowerShell module. This module is automatically installed on a computer when you install Azure AD Connect.

To view the current configuration of the scheduler, you can run the Get-ADSyncScheduler cmdlet. The output of this cmdlet is shown in Figure 4-28.

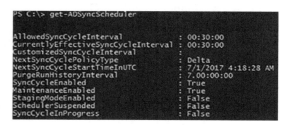

FIGURE 4-28 Get-ADSyncScheduler

The output of this cmdlet provides the following information:

- **AllowedSyncCyleInterval** Minimum intervals between sync cycles supported by Microsoft. If you sync more often than this interval, your configuration will be deemed unsupported.

- **CurrentlyEffectiveSyncCycleInterval** The schedule that currently applies.
- **CustomizedSyncCycleInterval** Used when you have a custom schedule applied.
- **NextSyncCyclePolicyType** Specifies whether the next sync is a full synchronization or a delta synchronization.
- **NextSyncCycleStartTimeInUTC** The time when the next sync cycle will occur according to the schedule.
- **PurgeRunHistoryInterval** Specifies how long the logs should be kept.
- **SyncCycleEnabled** Specifies whether the scheduler is running an import, sync, or export process as part of its execution.
- **MaintenanceEnabled** Specifies if the maintenance process is enabled.
- **StatingModeEnaled** Lists whether staging mode is enabled.
- **SyncCycleInProgress** Specifies whether synchronization is actually occurring.

You can use the Set-ADSyncScheduler cmdlet to configure the following settings that are displayed when you run the Get-ADSyncScheduler cmdlet:

- CustomizedSyncCycleInterval
- NextSyncCyclePolicyType
- PurgeRunHistoryInterval
- SyncCycleEnabled
- MaintenanceEnabled

> **MORE INFO MANAGING THE SCHEDULER**
>
> You can learn more about managing the Azure AD Connect scheduler at *https://docs.microsoft.com/en-us/azure/active-directory/connect/active-directory-aadconnectsync-feature-scheduler.*

Forcing synchronization

By default, synchronization occurs every 30 minutes. In some cases you'll make a change to a user account or create a collection of user accounts and want to get those changes or new accounts up into the Azure Active Directory instance that supports the Office 365 tenancy as fast as possible. You can force synchronization by just running the Azure AD Connect wizard again, or you can use the Synchronization Service Manager.

To perform a full synchronization using Synchronization Service Manager, perform the following steps.

1. Open Synchronization Service Manager, either by clicking on Synchronization Service from the Start menu or directly by running miisclient.exe located in the C:\Program Files\Microsoft Azure AD Sync\UIShell folder.

2. Click the Connectors tab.

3. On the Connectors tab, click the name of your Active Directory domain service as shown in Figure 4-29.

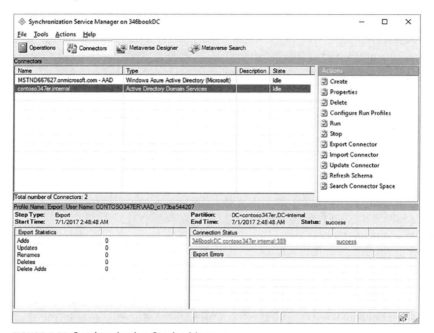

FIGURE 4-29 Synchronization Service Manager

4. On the Actions pane, click Run.

5. On the Run Management Agent dialog box, select Full Synchronization, as shown in Figure 4-30.

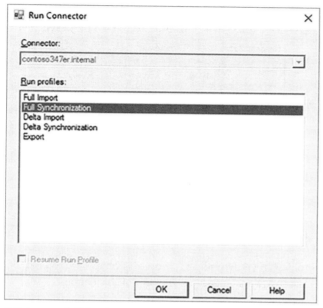

FIGURE 4-30 Full Synchronization

Rather than performing a Full Sync, you can trigger one of the following types of synchronization using the Synchronization Service Manager:

- **Full Synchronization**   Performs a full synchronization
- **Delta Import**   Imports changed schema and objects
- **Delta Synchronization**   Synchronizes only objects changed since the last sync
- **Export**   Writes data from the Azure instance to the on-premises instance
- **Full Import**   A full import and full sync is suitable for initiating the first full synchronization or the first full synchronization after you have changed the filtering parameters

You can also use Synchronization Service Manager to configure extensive filtering options, though for tasks such as configuring OU based filtering, Microsoft recommends that you first attempt configuring filtering using the Azure AD Connect setup wizard and only rely on a tool such as Synchronization Service Manager if problems arise.

> **MORE INFO** **SYNCHRONIZATION SERVICE MANAGER**
>
> You can learn more about Synchronization Service Manager at: *https://docs.microsoft.com/en-us/azure/active-directory/connect/active-directory-aadconnectsync-service-manager-ui.*

You can also force synchronization by using the Start-ADSyncCycle cmdlet. You can use this cmdlet to trigger either a delta or a full synchronization. To force a delta sync cycle, run the following command:

```
Start-ADSyncCycle -PolicyType Delta
```

To trigger a full sync cycle, run the command:

```
Start-ADSyncCycle -PolicyType Initial
```

EXAM TIP

Remember what tools you can use to force synchronization.

Thought experiment

In this thought experiment, apply what you've learned about this objective. You can find the answers to these questions in the "Answers" section at the end of this chapter.

You are in the process of consulting for Adatum about their planned synchronization solution that will allow them to replicate user account, group account, and mail enabled contacts from their on-premises Active Directory environment to an Azure Active Directory instance that supports an Office 365 tenancy. The Adatum environment consists of three forests with 21 separate domains. A preliminary assessment using the IdFix tool has found that it is necessary to make bulk changes to certain attributes used with user accounts before synchronization between the on-premises environment and Azure Active Directory can commence. Prior to full scale deployment of synchronization, it will also be necessary to have robust recovery procedures in the event that one or more accounts is deleted. Finally, all accounts at Adatum are in geography based OUs. Attributes, such as the Department attribute, denote the departments that the users are associated with.

With this in mind, answer the following questions:

1. How many instances of Azure AD Connect are necessary to sync the Adatum environment to a single Azure AD instance?

2. What tool, besides Microsoft PowerShell, could be used to bulk modify the attributes of selected user accounts at Adatum?

3. How can you ensure that members of the Research department don't have their accounts synchronized to the Azure Active Directory instance that supports the Office 365 tenancy?

4. What feature can you enable on the on-premises Active Directory instance that will allow you to recover an accidentally deleted account without having to recreate it with a new GUID?

5. How long are objects deleted from the Azure Active Directory instance used to support Office 365 recoverable?

Thought experiment answers

This section contains the solution to the thought experiment. Each answer explains why the answer choice is correct.

1. You only need a single instance of Azure AD Connect to synchronize from three separate Active Directory forests.

2. ADModify.NET can be used to bulk modify the attributes of selected user accounts at Adatum.

3. You can configure Azure AD Connect to only replicate specific OUs. You could also use tools such as the Synchronization Rules editor if more complicated synchronization rules are necessary.

4. Enabling Active Directory Recycle Bin allows you to recover an accidentally deleted account without having to recreate it with a new GUID.

5. Objects are recoverable from the Azure Active Directory Recycle Bin for 30 days.

Chapter summary

- Azure AD Connect is a tool that allows the replication of user accounts, groups, and mail enabled contacts from an on-premises Active Directory instance to an Azure Active Directory instance that supports the Office 365 tenancy.

- Prior to deploying Azure AD Connect, you should run a tool named IdFix to locate objects in the on-premises Active Directory that have attribute configurations that are incompatible with Azure AD Connect.

- If your organization has a non-routable domain, you'll need to update the UPN suffixes used by the accounts that you wish to synchronize to Azure Active Directory so that they use routable domain records.

- You can use Azure AD Connect to sync multiple Active Directory Forest to a single Azure Active Directory instance.

- Filtering allows you to control which user account, group account, and mail enabled contact objects are replicated to the Azure Active Directory instance that supports the Office 365 tenancy.

- Password Synchronization allows users to use the password they use with their on-premises Active Directory user account to sign into Office 365.

- When you configure Azure AD Connect, the source of authority for objects created in the on-premises Active Directory environment remains the on-premises Active Directory environment.

- When you create new users in the on-premises Active Directory environment and they are within the filtering scope of Azure AD Connect, accounts for these users will be created in the Azure Active Directory instance that supports the Office 365 tenancy the next time synchronization occurs.

- Modifications made to user accounts and groups using the on-premises tools will only apply to the counterpart objects in the Azure Active Directory instance that supports the Office 365 tenancy after synchronization occurs.

- Users and groups that are deleted from the on-premises Active Directory instance will not be deleted from the Azure Active Directory instance that supports the Office 365 tenancy until synchronization occurs.

- Objects that are accidentally deleted from the on-premises Active Directory can be recovered from the on-premises Active Directory Recycle Bin if it is enabled.

- You can force synchronization using the Synchronization Service Manager or Microsoft PowerShell.

CHAPTER 5

Implement and manage federated identities single sign on

You can configure single sign on for Office 365 by configuring federation between your on-premises Active Directory environment and Office 365 using Active Directory Federation Services. To configure single sign on, it is necessary to first configure an on-premises Active Directory Federation Services deployment, which includes servers hosting the AD FS role and the Web Application Proxy role. It is then necessary to link that on-premises AD FS deployment with Office 365.

Skills in this chapter:

- Skill 5.1: Plan requirements for Active Directory Federation Services
- Skill 5.2: Install and manage AD FS Servers
- Skill 5.3: Install and manage AD FS Proxy Servers

Skill 5.1: Plan requirements for Active Directory Federation Services

This objective deals with planning the configuration of the infrastructure required for deploying an Active Directory Federation Services (AD FS) instance to support configuring federation with Office 365. To master this objective, you'll need to understand the requirements for certificates used when configuring federation, the namespace, and network configuration requirements. You'll also need to know what steps you need to take to implement multi-factor authentication in an environment where you have configured single sign on. You'll also need to know what parts need to be configured to set up access filtering using claims rules.

Deploying AD FS topologies

How you deploy AD FS to work with Office 365 depends on the number of users that need to perform single sign on operations. The most basic form of AD FS deployment is that you place a server on your internal network running Windows Server 2012 R2 with the AD FS role installed and configured. You then place at least one server on your organization's perimeter network that functions as a proxy, relaying traffic between the AD FS server on the internal network and the Office 365 infrastructure.

EXAM TIP

In Windows Server 2012 R2, the AD FS Proxy server role was modified to become the Web Application Proxy server role. You'll need to remember that the term AD FS Proxy is the term used when working with computers running Windows Server 2008, Windows Server 2008 R2, and Windows Server 2012, and that Web Application Proxy is the term used with computers running Windows Server 2012 R2 and Windows Server 2016.

AD FS is a role service that is available with Windows Server. Microsoft has released the following versions of AD FS:

- **AD FS 1.0**   Released with Windows Server 2003 R2
- **AD FS 1.1**   Released with Windows Server 2008 and Windows Server 2008 R2
- **AD FS 2.0**. Released as a separate download for Windows Server 2008 and Windows Server 2008 R2
- **AD FS 2.1**   Released with Windows Server 2012
- **AD FS 3.0**   Released with Windows Server 2012 R2
- **AD FS 4.0**   Released with Windows Server 2016

An internal AD FS deployment is termed a farm. In versions of AD FS prior to version 3, released with Windows Server 2012 R2, you could choose to deploy AD FS as a standalone or as a farm. With AD FS version 3, you always install AD FS as a farm. The key to understanding AD FS farms is that an AD FS farm can consist of a single server.

Microsoft makes the following recommendations with respect to the number of AD FS servers that you should deploy in an environment.

- **Fewer than 1,000 users** Deploy a single AD FS server in a farm. Deploy a single Web Application Proxy server on the perimeter network.
- **1,000 to 15,000 users** Deploy two AD FS servers in a farm. Deploy two load balanced web application proxy servers on the perimeter network.
- **15,000 to 60,000 users** Deploy between three and five AD FS servers in a farm. Deploy two load balanced Web Application Proxy servers on the perimeter network.

> **MORE INFO AD FS DEPLOYMENT TOPOLOGIES**
>
> You can learn more about AD FS deployment topologies at: *https://technet.microsoft.com/en-us/library/dn554241.aspx.*

Using certificates

Certificates verify the identity of each element of an AD FS deployment. Certificates are also used to secure communication across computers hosting the AD FS Federation Server roles, computers hosting the Web Application Proxy role, as well as the Office 365 servers.

The Service Communications Certificate is the certificate that you install for the purpose of service identification and secure communication. This certificate is a server authentication certificate, occasionally called an Secure Sockets Layer (SSL) certificate, a Transport Layer Security (TLS) certificate, or web server certificate.

Federation server certificate requirements

Computers that host the federation server role have different certificate requirements depending on whether they are running AD FS 3.0 on Windows Server 2012 R2 or AD FS 4.0 on Windows Server 2016 or have a previous version of AD FS running on an earlier version of Windows Server.

If the AD FS Federation Server is running the Windows Server 2012 R2 or Windows Server 2016 operating system, it requires a Service Communications Certificate as shown in Figure 5-1. The Service Communications Certificate is a server authentication certificate, also known more colloquially as an SSL certificate.

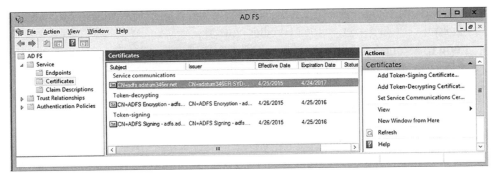

FIGURE 5-1 AD FS Service Communications Certificate

The Service Communications Certificate must have the following properties:

■ The certificates' Subject Name and Subject Alternative Name must include the federation service name. For example, adfs.adatum346ER.net.

■ The certificate's Subject Alternative Name must contain the value enterpriseregistration and the UPN suffix of the organization. For example, enterpriseregistration. adatum346ER.net.

■ Certificate cannot be a wildcard certificate.

■ It is necessary to have both the certificate and the private key when running the Active Directory Federation Services Configuration Wizard.

■ Certificate must be issued by a trusted third party certification authority.

There are a variety of methods that you can use to request a certificate depending on which CA you are using to request the certificate from. Publicly trusted CAs have web forms that allow you to submit a certificate request. You need to use a public CA to obtain the certificate, because Microsoft's Office 365 servers cannot be configured by tenants to trust a certificate from an internal CA.

EXAM TIP

Although you cannot use a certificate generated from an internal Enterprise CA to connect to Office 365, you can perform many of the steps required to configure AD FS using this certificate. For the purposes of exam preparation, this may present a reasonable alternative for those not wishing to go to the expense of purchasing a domain name and a certificate to study for a single objective domain on a certification exam.

For the purposes of demonstrating what is required to request a certificate from a CA, the certificate request process is demonstrated using an internal Enterprise CA. An enterprise CA is used because each public CA has a separate process for requesting certificates. To request a certificate that has the appropriate properties using the Certificates console from an Enterprise CA, perform the following steps.

1. Sign on to the computer that will host the AD FS role using an account that has local Administrator privileges.

2. Right-click the Start hint and click Run.

3. In the Run dialog box, type mmc.exe as shown in Figure 5-2 and click OK.

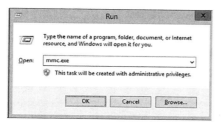

FIGURE 5-2 Run dialog box

4. On the File menu of the Console1 – [Console Root] dialog box, click Add/Remove Snap-in.

5. On the Add Or Remove Snap-ins dialog box, click Certificates as shown in Figure 5-3, and then click Add.

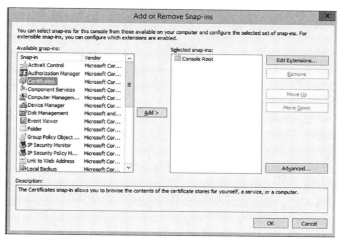

FIGURE 5-3 Certificates snap in

6. On the Certificates snap-in dialog box, shown in Figure 5-4, click Computer Account and click Next.

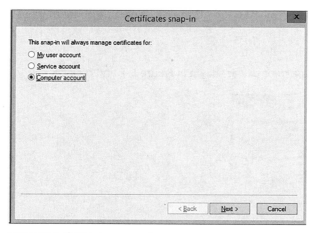

FIGURE 5-4 Computer account

7. On the Select Computer page, ensure that Local Computer is selected as shown in Figure 5-5 and then click Finish.

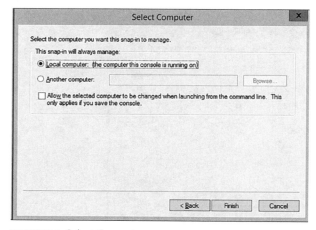

FIGURE 5-5 Select Computer

8. Click OK to close the Add or Remove Snap-ins dialog box.

9. On the Consol1 – [Console Root] dialog box, expand the Certificates (Local Computer) node and then select the Personal node as shown in Figure 5-6.

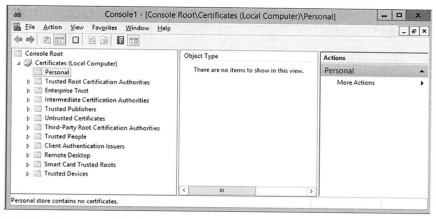

FIGURE 5-6 Personal certificates store

10. On the Action menu, click All Tasks, and then click Request New Certificate.

11. On the Before You Begin page of the Certificate Enrollment wizard, click Next.

12. On the Select Certificate Enrollment Policy dialog box, ensure that Active Directory Enrollment Policy is selected as shown in Figure 5-7 and click Next.

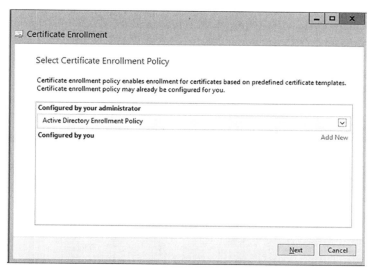

FIGURE 5-7 Enrollment Policy

13. On the Request Certificate page, select Web Server as shown in Figure 5-8 and then click More Information Is Required To Enroll For This Certificate, Click Here To Configure Settings. If the Web Server certificate template is not available, you must ensure that the computer account of the AD FS server is configured with enrollment permissions on the certificate template. You can do this using the Certificate Templates console on an Enterprise CA.

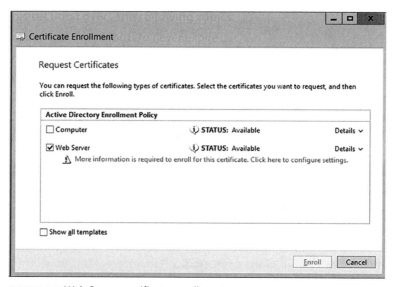

FIGURE 5-8 Web Server certificate enrollment

14. On the Certificate Properties dialog box, set the Type to Common Name, enter the fully qualified domain name of the Federation Service name (which is separate from the fully qualified domain name of the AD FS server), and then click Add. Figure 5-9 shows this as adfs.adatum345er.net.

FIGURE 5-9 Common Name setting

15. Under alternative name, set the Type to DNS and then enter the value enterpriseregistration with the UPN suffix of the organization and then click Add. Figure 5-10 shows this as enterpriseregistration.adatum346er.net.

FIGURE 5-10 Alternative name

16. Click OK to close the Certificate Properties dialog box.

17. On the Certificate Enrollment dialog box, shown in Figure 5-11, click Enroll.

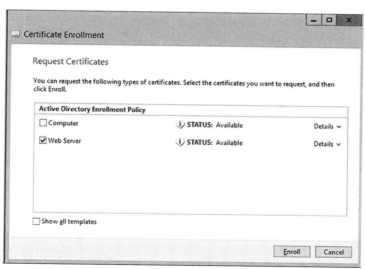

FIGURE 5-11 Web Server certificate

18. On the Certificate Installation Results page, click Finish.

Once you have received the certificate from a CA and installed it on the computer that hosts the AD FS role, you should export the certificate, including exporting the private key, so that you can use the certificate when configuring the web application proxy server or when adding additional AD FS servers to the farm.

To export the private key, perform the following steps:

1. In the Console1 – Console Root console, with the Certificates (Local Computer) snap-in added, navigate to the Personal\Certificates node, and select the certificate. Figure 5-12 shows the adfs.adatum346er.net certificate selected.

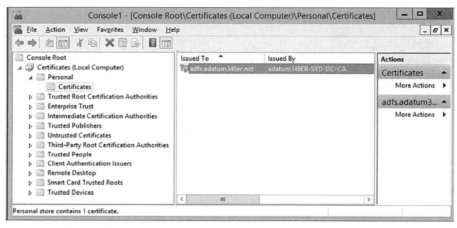

FIGURE 5-12 Installed certificate

2. On the Action menu, click All Tasks and then click Export.

3. On the Welcome To The Certificate Export Wizard page of the Certificate Export Wizard, click Next.

4. On the Export Private Key page, select Yes, Export The Private Key as shown in Figure 5-13. If this option is not available, you need to update the Certificate Template on the Enterprise CA so that you are able to export private keys and then request a new certificate.

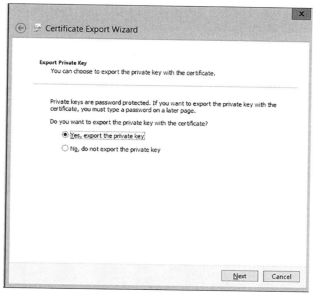

FIGURE 5-13 Export Private Key

5. On the Export File Format page of the Certificate Export Wizard, ensure that you select the Include All Certificates In The Certificate Path If Possible option, and the Export All Extended Properties option as shown in Figure 5-14. Ensure that you do not select the Delete The Private Key If The Export Is Successful Option. Click Next.

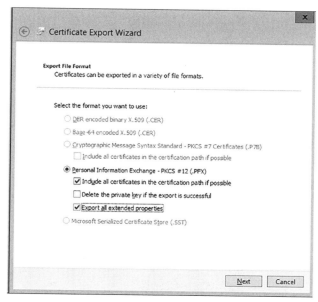

FIGURE 5-14 Export file format

6. On the Security page, select the Password option and then provide a password to protect the certificate as shown in Figure 5-15.

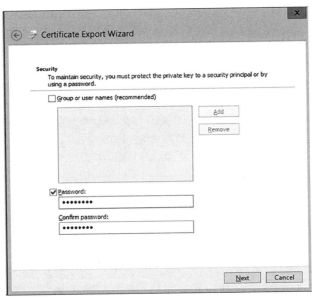

FIGURE 5-15 Export security

7. On the File To Export page of the Certificate Export Wizard, select a location to save the exported certificate as shown in Figure 5-16 and then click Next.

FIGURE 5-16 File to Export

8. On the Completing the Certificate Export Wizard page, click Finish.

If the AD FS Federation Server is running a version of AD FS prior to AD FS 3.0, the Service Communications Certificate requirements differ compared to the requirements if the AD FS server is running AD FS 3.0 or AD FS 4.0. These requirements are as follows:

- The certificate requires the Subject Name to be a short name, rather than a fully qualified domain name.

- This certificate must be trusted by Microsoft cloud services as well as AD FS clients. This means that it needs to be issued by a trusted third-party CA.

- The certificate cannot be a wildcard certificate.

The AD FS server needs a token signing certificate. The token signing certificate is an X.509 certificate. This certificate is used to sign the tokens issued by the federation server that the cloud service accepts and validates. The default is that you use the self-signed token-signing certificate that generated by AD FS for this task rather than generating a certificate from a CA. The advantage of using a self-signed token-signing certificate is that AD FS automatically manage the certificate, meaning that this specific certificate will require no intervention on the part of the AD FS administrator in future.

Adhering to Web Application Proxy certificate requirements

The computer that hosts the Web Application Proxy, the AD FS Proxy in previous versions of Windows Server, requires a server authentication certificate that has the same subject name as the server authentication certificate installed on the computer that hosts the AD FS role. This certificate must be imported into the Personal Certificates store of the computer that hosts the Web Application Proxy role. If you are using a computer that has an operating system running Windows Server 2008, Windows Server 2008 R2, or Windows Server 2012 that is functioning as a federation proxy server, this server authentication certificate must be installed on the Default Web Site of the computer that hosts the federation proxy server role.

> **MORE INFO AD FS CERTIFICATE REQUIREMENTS**
>
> You can learn more about AD FS Certificate Requirements at: *https://docs.microsoft.com/ en-us/windows-server/identity/ad-fs/overview/ad-fs-2016-requirements*.

Using namespaces

The name of the AD FS service must be resolvable through external DNS. For example, if the name of your AD FS service is adfs.adatum346er.net, clients on the Internet must be able to resolve this name using a DNS server on the Internet. This means that the name must be configured as a host record in the appropriate publicly accessible DNS zone. Microsoft recommends using a host (A) record for the AD FS service rather than using a CNAME that points to another record. This is because in some circumstances using a CNAME record rather than a

HOST record can cause authentication issues, because Kerberos tickets may be issued to the incorrect name.

Kerberos is used to identify the AD FS service on the internal network. This occurs through the service's Service Principal Name (SPN). The AD FS SPN is set automatically when running the AD FS configuration wizard.

Meeting network requirements

To ensure that you can configure federation between your on premises Active Directory instance and Office 365, you must ensure that the following network requirements are met:

- TCP/IP connectivity must exist between the Internet and the Web Application Proxy servers on the perimeter network. This allows communication between Microsoft's Office 365 servers and the computers hosting the Web Application Proxy role.

- For external clients, the fully qualified domain name of the AD FS service must resolve to the public IP address of the Web Application Proxy server. For example, if the AD FS service name is adfs.adatum346er.net, then this address must resolve to the public IP address of the web application proxy server. If you have configured load balancing for the Web Application Proxy servers, then this address will need to resolve to the public IP address of the load balancer.

> **MORE INFO NETWORK REQUIREMENTS**
>
> You can learn more about network requirements at: *https://docs.microsoft.com/en-us/windows-server/identity/ad-fs/overview/ad-fs-2016-requirements#BKMK_7.*

Configuring multi-factor authentication

You can configure AD FS on Windows Server 2012 R2 and Windows Server 2016 to support Multi-Factor authentication by downloading and installing the Azure Multi-Factor Authentication Server. This server can be downloaded from the Microsoft Azure portal and installed either on a server with the AD FS role installed or on a separate computer that is a member of the same domain.

When installed, you can configure the multi-factor authentication server so that users are allowed to select their multi-factor authentication method. You can use the following methods for multi-factor authentication:

- Phone call
- Text message
- Mobile app
- OATH Token

You can also configure a specific number of security questions as a fallback option. Figure 5-17 shows the Phone Call, Text Message, and Mobile App methods selected.

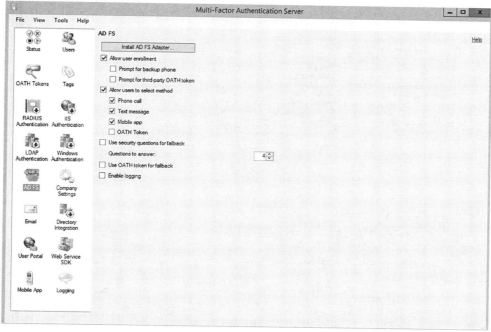

FIGURE 5-17 Multi-factor authentication server

When configured, users will be required to use two forms of authentication when accessing Office 365 resources when using single sign on.

MORE INFO MFA AND AD FS

You can learn more about integrating Multi-Factor Authentication with Windows Server 2012 R2 AD FS and Office 365 at: *https://docs.microsoft.com/en-us/azure/multi-factor-authentication/multi-factor-authentication-get-started-adfs-w2k12.*

Accessing filtering using claims rules

By configuring the claim rules after you have configured federation between your on-premises Active Directory environment and Office 365, you can block access to Office 365 depending on the properties of the account making the claim. For example, you can block access to Office 365 for users when they are located on networks outside the organization, but allow the same users access to Office 365 when they are using a computer located on an organizational network. You do this by editing the claims rules for Active Directory using the AD FS console as shown in Figure 5-18.

FIGURE 5-18 Claims Rules

MORE INFO **ACCESS FILTERING USING CLAIM RULES**

You can learn more about access filtering using claim rules found at: *https://technet. microsoft.com/en-us/library/hh526961%28v=ws.10%29.aspx.*

Skill 5.2: Install and manage AD FS Servers

This objective deals with installing and managing an Active Directory Federation Services server farm. To master this objective you'll need to understand the requirements of configuring the AD FS service account, configuring a farm, adding servers to a farm, converting an Office 365 domain from standard to federated, and managing the certificate lifecycle.

> **This section covers the following topics:**
>
> - Create AD FS service accounts
> - Configure farm or stand-alone settings
> - Add additional servers
> - Convert from standard to federated domain
> - Manage certificate life cycle

Creating AD FS service accounts

AD FS requires a dedicated service account. You create this service account before configuring the first AD FS server in a farm. When you add the first server to the farm, or add additional servers, you provide the credentials of this service account.

EXAM TIP

Remember that you will need to provide the same service account credentials each time you add a new server running the AD FS role to an existing AD FS farm.

This account should be configured with the following properties:

- The password should be configured to not expire, as shown in Figure 5-19.

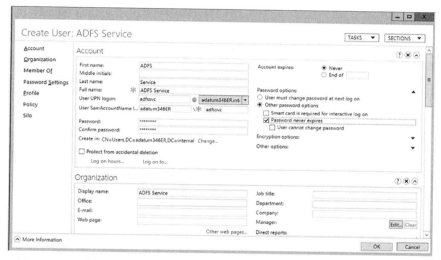

FIGURE 5-19 Service account configured with the Password Never Expires option

- Ensure that the account has the Log On As A Service right on computers hosting the AD FS role. You can configure this right through group policy as shown in Figure 5-20.

FIGURE 5-20 Service account configured with the Log On As A Service right

■ Ensure that the account has the Log On As A Batch Job right on computers hosting the AD FS role. You can configure this right through group policy as shown in Figure 5-21.

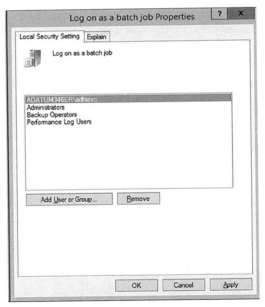

FIGURE 5-21 Service account configured with the Log On As A Batch Job right

When you run the AD FS Configuration Wizard and specify the service account, the AD FS configuration process will automatically configure the appropriate Service Principal Names (SPN).

You can use the setspn.exe command line tool if you want to register the SPN manually. To do this, you use the command with the following format:

```
Setspn.exe -a host/<server name> <service account>
```

For example, to configure the SPN for the server adfs.adatum346er.net for the service account adfssvc, issue the following command using an account that has domain administrator privileges:

```
Setspn.exe -a host/adfs.adatum346er.net adfssvc
```

> **MORE INFO AD FS SERVICE ACCOUNT**
>
> You can learn more about configuring a service account for AD FS at: *https://docs.micro-soft.com/en-us/windows-server/identity/ad-fs/deployment/manually-configure-a-service-account-for-a-federation-server-farm.*

With AD FS in Windows Server 2012 R2 and Windows Server 2016, you have the option of using a group managed service account. Group managed service accounts have their passwords managed by Active Directory. This makes them more secure than a manually created account configured so that the password never expires. Group Managed Service Accounts require that at least one domain controller in the domain is running Windows Server 2012 or later.

> **MORE INFO GROUP MANAGED SERVICE ACCOUNTS**
>
> You can learn more about group managed service accounts at: *https://technet.microsoft.com/en-us/library/jj128431.aspx.*

Configuring farm or stand-alone settings

In versions of AD FS prior to version 3.0, which is included with Windows Server 2012 R2, you were asked, during deployment, to choose whether you wanted to configure the AD FS deployment as a farm or in a stand-alone configuration. The drawback of choosing the stand-alone configuration was that you were tied to that decision and couldn't convert the deployment to a farm if your requirements changed. As it was possible to deploy a single server farm, most advice was to deploy versions prior to 3.0 in the farm configuration as it gives you flexibility to expand the deployment at a later point in time.

With AD FS 3.0 on Windows Server 2012 R2 and AD FS 4.0 on Windows Server 2016, there is no longer the option to deploy a standalone server and you always deploy AD FS as part of a farm. The only choice that an administrator is presented with is whether you will be deploying the AD FS server as the first server in a new farm, or as an additional server in an existing farm. Figure 5-22 shows the Active Directory Federation Services Configuration Wizard that displays this option.

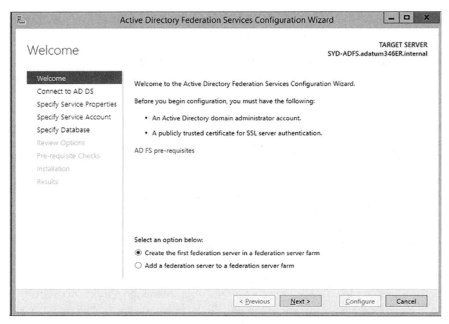

FIGURE 5-22 Create a new farm or add a server to an existing farm

---

MORE INFO ADDING AD FS SERVER

You can learn more about adding the first federation server in a farm at: *https://docs. microsoft.com/en-us/windows-server/identity/ad-fs/deployment/configure-a-federation-server.*

Installing and configuring AD FS

The AD FS role must be installed on a computer that is joined to a domain. The AD FS role can be installed on a computer that hosts the domain controller role. There are two steps to installing the role: the first is to install the role and the second is to configure the role. Prior to installing and configuring the role, you should create and configure a service account. You also need to have acquired the appropriate server authentication certificate.

To install the role on a computer running the Windows Server 2012 R2 or Windows Server 2016 operating system, perform the following steps:

1. In the Server Manager console, select the Dashboard node and then select Add Roles and Features.

2. On the Before You Begin page of the Add Roles and Features wizard, click Next.

3. On the Installation Type page, select Role-Based or Feature-Based Installation as shown in Figure 5-23, click Next.

FIGURE 5-23 Role-based or feature-based installation

4. On the Select Destination Server page, ensure that the local server is selected. Figure 5-24 shows the server SYD-ADFS.adatum346er.internal selected. Click Next.

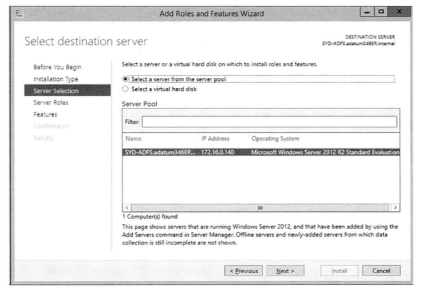

FIGURE 5-24 Select destination server

5. On the Select Server Roles page, select Active Directory Federation Services as shown in Figure 5-25 and then click Next.

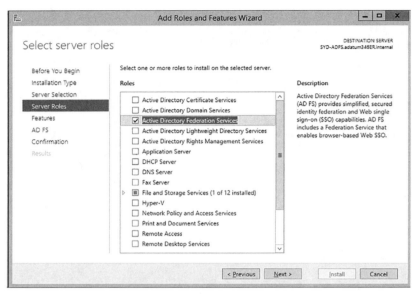

FIGURE 5-25 Select Active Directory Federation Services

6. On the Select Features page, click Next.

7. On the Active Directory Federation Services (AD FS) page, review the information as shown in Figure 5-26 and then click Next.

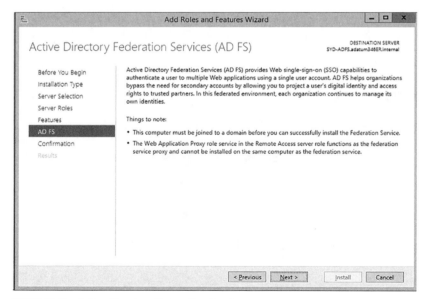

FIGURE 5-26 Active Directory Federation Services

8. On the Confirmation page, select the Restart The Destination Server Automatically If Required checkbox and then click Install.

9. Click Close to close the Add Roles and Features Wizard.

To configure the first server in a farm, perform the following steps:

10. On the Server Manager console, click the AD FS node.

11. With the AD FS node of the Server Manager console selected, click the text that says More next to Configuration Required for Active Directory Federation Services as shown in Figure 5-27.

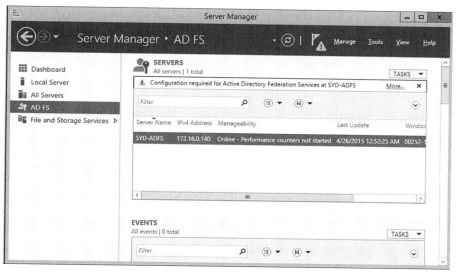

FIGURE 5-27 Server Manager console

12. On the All Servers Tasks Details dialog box, shown in Figure 5-28, click Configure the Federation Service.

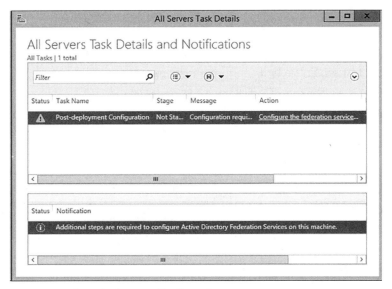

FIGURE 5-28 Post-deployment Configuration

13. On the Welcome page of the Active Directory Federation Services Configuration Wizard, ensure that Create The First Federation Server In A Federation Server Farm is selected as shown in Figure 5-29 and click Next.

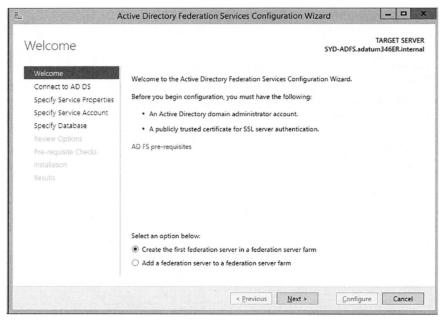

FIGURE 5-29 Create the first federation server in a server farm

14. On the Connect To AD DS page, shown in Figure 5-30, provide the credentials of a user account that has domain administrator permissions. Click Next.

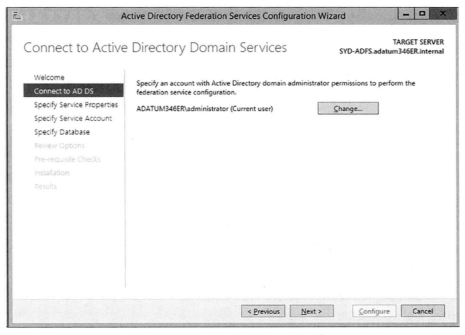

FIGURE 5-30 Provide domain administrator credentials

15. On the Specify Service Properties page, select the Server Authentication certificate that will be used to identify the ADFS service. You should also provide a display name as shown in Figure 5-31. The Federation Service Name will be taken from the Subject Name of the Server Authentication certificate, also termed the SSL Certificate. Click Next.

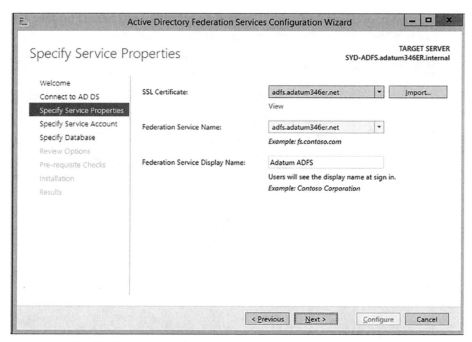

FIGURE 5-31 Specify Service Properties

16. On the Specify Service Account name page, you can have the AD FS Configuration Wizard create a Group Managed Service Account if the KDS Root Key has been configured and there is at least one domain controller running Windows Server 2012 or later in the domain. As an alternative, you can configure a service account with the appropriate rights and settings as outlined earlier in this chapter. Figure 5-32 shows the service account configured earlier in this chapter named ADATUM346ER\adfssvc. If manually specifying a service account, you will need to provide the service account password.

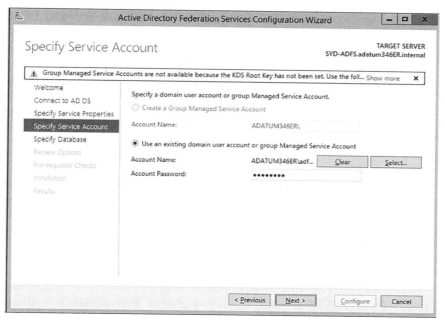

FIGURE 5-32 Specify Service Properties

17. On the Specify Database page, choose between an existing SQL Server instance or having AD FS create a Windows Internal Database instance. Microsoft recommends using a SQL Server instance if the AD FS server experiences performance problems when using the Windows Internal Database. It is possible to migrate from the Windows Internal Database to a separate SQL Server instance using SQL Server Management Studio. Figure 5-33 shows the Specify Configuration Database page.

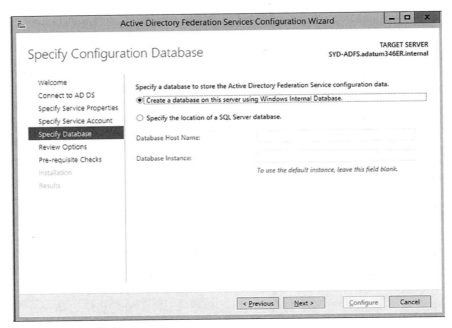

FIGURE 5-33 Specify Configuration Database

18. On the Review Options page, shown in 5-34, review the configuration options.

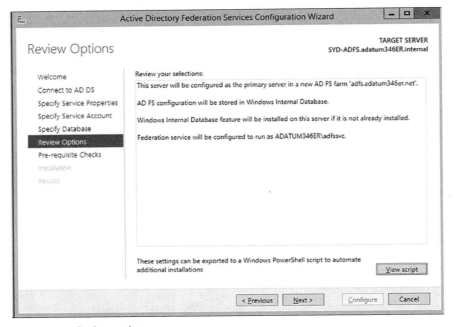

FIGURE 5-34 Review options

19. You also have the option on this page of clicking View Script. This will provide you with a PowerShell script to add additional servers with the AD FS role to the farm. Figure 5-35 shows an example of this script.

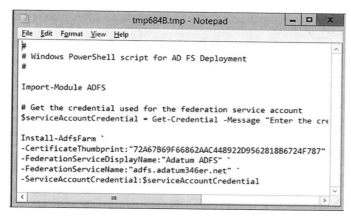

FIGURE 5-35 Installation script

20. On the Pre-requisite Checks page, ensure that all pre-requisite checks are passed successfully, as shown in Figure 5-36 and then click Configure.

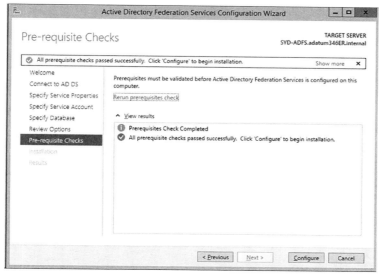

FIGURE 5-36 Pre-requisite checks

21. Click Close to complete the Active Directory Federation Services Configuration Wizard.

MORE INFO INSTALLING THE FIRST AD FS SERVER

You can learn more about installing and integrating AD FS with Office 365 at: *http://blogs. technet.com/b/rmilne/archive/2014/04/28/how-to-install-adfs-2012-r2-for-office-365.aspx.*

Adding additional servers

You can add additional AD FS servers to the farm as required. Microsoft recommends that if your organization needs to support more than 1,000 federated users, you should deploy two dedicated federation servers. For each additional 15,000 users, Microsoft recommends adding an additional Federation Server.

When you deploy AD FS using the Windows Internal Database, the first server deployed in the farm has read and write access to that database. Additional AD FS servers deployed to the farm store read only copies using their own Windows Internal Database instance. If the first server deployed in the farm fails, one of the other servers in the farm can be promoted so that it has read and write access to the database.

If you deploy AD FS using a SQL Server instance, all servers in the farm have read and write access to the database. The drawback of doing this is that it requires that the SQL Server is licensed appropriately.

To prepare a server to become an additional AD FS server in the farm, including importing the appropriate certificate and assigning the AD FS service account the appropriate rights, perform the following steps:

1. Install the Active Directory Federation Services binaries using the method outlined earlier, or by issuing the following Windows PowerShell command:

    ```
    Install-WindowsFeature –IncludeManagementTools ADFS-Federation
    -IncludeManagementTools
    ```

2. Ensure that the AD FS Service Communications Certificate is installed in the personal certificate store of the computer account. You can do this by copying the exported certificate across to the computer that you want to add to the AD FS farm and then double clicking on it to run the Certificate Import Wizard. On the Welcome to the Certificate Import Wizard page of the Certificate Import Wizard, click Local Machine as shown in Figure 5-37 and then click Next.

FIGURE 5-37 Import the Certificate to the Local Machine certificate store

3. On the Specify The File You Want To Import, verify that the exported certificate file is present as shown in Figure 5-38 and then click Next.

FIGURE 5-38 File to import

4. On the Private Key Protection page, provide the certificate password, and ensure that the key is marked as exportable, and that you want to include all extended properties as shown in Figure 5-39. Click Next.

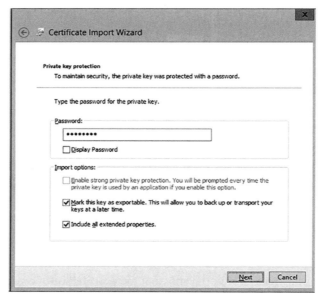

FIGURE 5-39 Private key protection

5. On the Certificate Store page, click Place All Certificates In The Following Store and then click Browse.

6. On the Select Certificate Store dialog box, select Personal as shown in Figure 5-40 and then click OK.

FIGURE 5-40 Select Certificate Store

7. Verify that the Certificate Store page of the Certificate Import Wizard matches Figure 5-41 and then click Next.

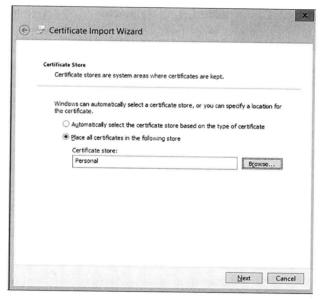

FIGURE 5-41 Certificate Store

8. On the Completing the Certificate Import Wizard page, click Finish.

9. Right-click the Start hint and then click Run.

10. In the Run dialog box, type **gpedit.msc** as shown in Figure 5-42 and then click OK.

FIGURE 5-42 Open the local Group Policy editor

11. In the Local Group Policy Editor, navigate to the Computer Configuration\Windows Settings\Security Settings\Local Policies\User Rights Assignment node as shown in Figure 5-43.

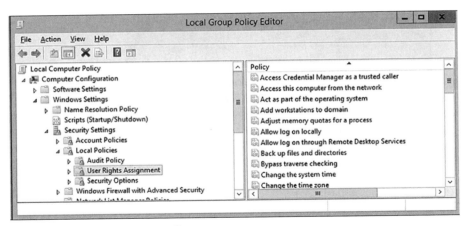

FIGURE 5-43 Local Group Policy Editor

12. In the Policy pane, double click Log on As a Batch Job.

13. In the Log On As A Batch Job dialog box, click Add User or Group, and then add the service account used for the AD FS service. Click OK. Figure 5-44 shows the ADFSSVC account added. Click OK.

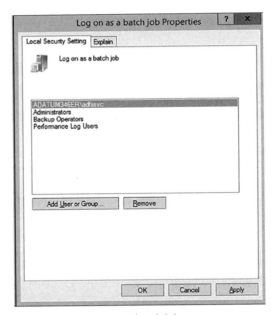

FIGURE 5-44 Log on as a batch job

14. Double click the Log On As A Service policy.

15. In the Log On As A Service Job dialog box, click Add User or Group and then add the service account used for the AD FS service. Click OK. Figure 5-45 shows the ADFSSVC account added. Click OK.

FIGURE 5-45 Log on as a service

16. Close the Group Policy editor.

17. Open a Windows PowerShell window and issue the following command:

```
Gpupdate /force
```

Once the AD FS Service Communications Certificate has been installed and the appropriate rights have been assigned to the service account, you can add the additional AD FS server to the farm by performing the following steps:

1. Click the AD FS node of the Server Manager console.

2. Next to the Configuration Required for Active Directory Federation Services notification, shown in Figure 5-46, click More.

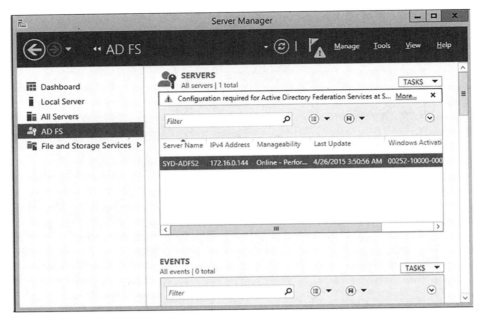

FIGURE 5-46 Configuration Required

3. On the All Server Task Details dialog box, shown in Figure 5-47, click Configure The Federation Service.

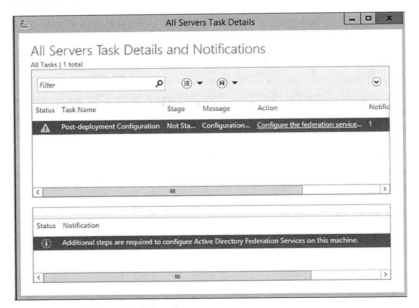

FIGURE 5-47 All Server Task Details

4. On the Welcome page of the Active Directory Federation Services Configuration Wizard, click Add A Federation Server To A Federation Server Farm, as shown in Figure 5-48 and then click Next.

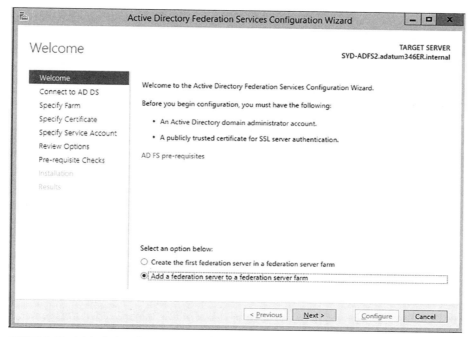

FIGURE 5-48   Add a federation server to a federation Server Farm

5. On the Connect To Active Directory Domain Services page, specify a user account that has Domain Administrator credentials as shown in Figure 5-49 and then click Next.

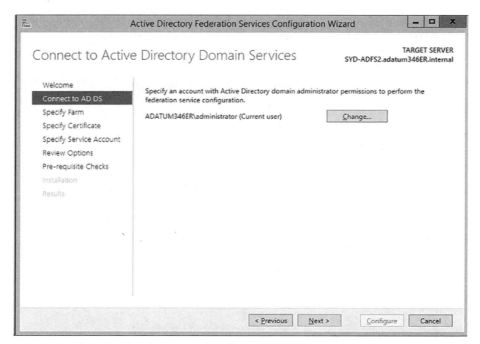

FIGURE 5-49 Domain Administrator credentials

6. On the Specify Farm page, specify the FQDN of the Primary Federation Server. The Primary Federation Server is the first AD FS server deployed in the farm. If you are using an SQL Server instance to support AD FS, you should instead specify the address of the SQL Server instance. Figure 5-50 shows the Primary Federation Server set to SYD-ADFS.adatum346ER.internal.

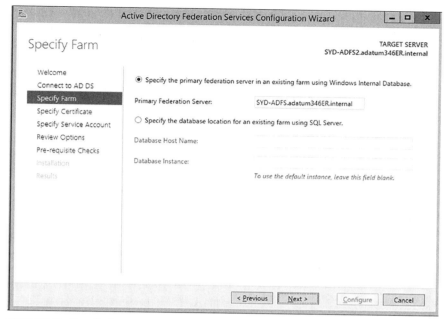

FIGURE 5-50 Specify Farm

7. On the Specify Certificate page, specify the imported AD FS service authentication certificate as shown in Figure 5-51.

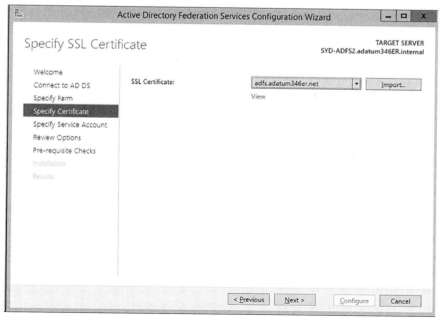

FIGURE 5-51 Specify Certificate

8. On the Specify Service Account page, specify the same service account that you con-figured when configuring the first Federation Server. If you are using an account you created yourself for this purpose, rather than a group managed service account, you will need to specify the password as shown in Figure 5-52.

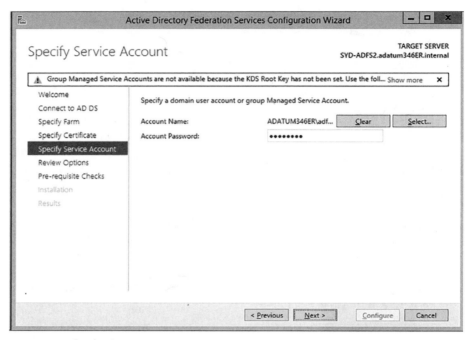

FIGURE 5-52 Service Account

9. On the Review Options page, review the options and then click Next.

10. On the Pre-requisite checks page, verify that the pre-requisite checks have completed successfully as shown in Figure 5-53 and then click Configure.

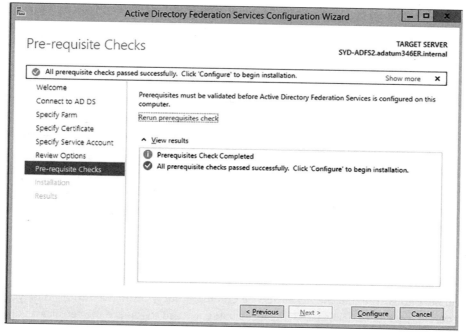

FIGURE 5-53 Service Account

11. On the Results page, click Close.

MORE INFO **ADDING ADDITIONAL AD FS SERVERS**

You can learn more about adding AD FS servers to an existing farm at: *https://technet.microsoft.com/en-us/library/e340cf8f-acf3-4cba-8135-a9353b85e714#BKMK_2.*

Converting from standard to federated domain

You convert an Office 365 domain from standard to Federated using cmdlets found in the Azure Active Directory PowerShell module. You can only perform the conversion once your AD FS deployment is functioning correctly, and you have deployed your Web Application Proxy server on the perimeter network to allow Office 365 to communicate with your internal AD FS deployment. You will learn more about deploying the Web Application Proxy server in the next lesson.

To convert from a standard to a federated domain, you first establish a connection from your Azure Active Directory PowerShell session to Office 365 using the Connect-MsolService cmdlet. Once you have presented your credentials, you provide information about the AD FS deployment by using the Set-MsolADFSContext cmdlet and specifying one of the AD FS servers. For example, to provide information about the server SYD-ADFS.adatum346er.net, use the following command.

```
Set-MsolADFSContext –Computer SYD-ADFS.adatum346er.net
```

Once the connection to Office 365 has been established and the AD FS context has been set, you can convert a domain to become Federated by running the command:

```
Convert-MsolDomainToFederated –DomainName Adatum346er.net
```

You can verify that the domain is now federated by using the Get-MsolDomain cmdlet. If you have been successful, the output of this cmdlet will identify the authentication for the domain as Federated. Domains that have not been converted will be listed as Managed.

> **MORE INFO** **CONVERTING TO FEDERATED DOMAIN**
>
> You can learn more about converting an Office 365 domain to a federated domain at:
> http://blogs.technet.com/b/rmilne/archive/2014/04/30/how-to-install-adfs-2012-r2-for-office-365-part-3.aspx.

Managing certificate life cycle

You need to ensure that the AD FS Service Communication Certificates installed on your Federation server remain valid. This means that you need to replace the certificates on each AD FS server in the farm before they expire. If you have configured the AD FS server to manage the token signing certificates, these will automatically be replaced. If you have configured manual management of the token signing certificates, a configuration which Microsoft doesn't recommend, you'll also have to replace these certificates before they expire.

You can replace the Service Communication Certificate, which is the server authentication certificate, also known as an SSL or web server certificate you specified when deploying AD FS by performing the following steps:

1. Ensure that you have installed the new Service Communication Certificate in the Personal Store of each AD FS server in the AD FS farm.

2. Click AD FS Management on the Tools menu of the Server Manager console.

3. In the AD FS console, click the Certificates node under the Service Node and then select the Service Communications certificate as shown in Figure 5-54.

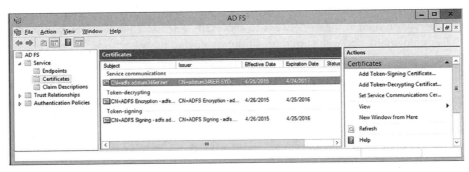

FIGURE 5-54 AD FS console

4. In the Actions pane, click Set Service Communications Certificate.

5. On the Windows Security dialog box, shown in Figure 5-55, select the Service Communications Certificate to use with AD FS and then click OK. You may be prompted with a warning about the private key being required on each AD FS server in the farm.

FIGURE 5-55 Select Service Communications Certificate

EXAM TIP

Remember which console you use to update the Service Communication Certificate. Also remember that the Token Signing and Token Decrypting Certificates are managed by AD FS and do not require manual replacement.

Skill 5.3: Install and manage AD FS Proxy Servers

This objective deals with installing and managing AD FS Proxy Servers. It's very important to remember that from Windows Server 2012 R2 onward, the role service known as AD FS Proxy Server has been renamed Web Application Server. To master this objective you'll need to understand what steps you need to take to set up perimeter network name resolution, what roles and features need to be deployed to install the Web Application Proxy, the properties of the certificate to install on the Web Application Proxy, and how to configure custom settings for the proxy login page.

This section covers the following topics:

■ Set up perimeter network name resolution

■ Install required Windows roles and features

■ Set up certificates

■ Configure AD FS Web Application Proxy

■ Set custom proxy forms login page

Setting up perimeter network name resolution

Microsoft recommends that for external name resolution you configure an A record that maps the public name of the AD FS service to the public IP address of the Web Application Proxy server on the perimeter network.

The needs of the Web Application Proxy server itself are a little different. The computer that will function as the proxy server itself needs to be able to resolve the address of the AD FS servers. You can perform this operation by configuring DNS if you are using a split DNS. An alternative is to configure the hosts file on each computer, mapping the name of the AD FS service to the IP addresses of each member of the AD FS server farm.

EXAM TIP

Remember that the name resolution requirement for the Web Application Proxy server is different to the name resolution requirements for the Office 365 servers. One requires resolution of the AD FS service name to the Web Application Proxy server, and the other requires name resolution to the AD FS servers on the internal network.

Setting up certificates

You need to install the AD FS Service Communications Certificate on each Web Application Proxy server. This certificate needs to be installed to the Computer account's Personal store as shown in Figure 5-56.

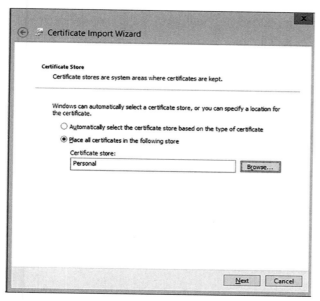

FIGURE 5-56 Import Service Communications Certificate

Installing required Windows roles and features

Installing the Web Application Proxy role involves installing the Remote Access role rather than the AD FS role. To install the Web Application Proxy role, perform the following steps:

1. In the Dashboard node of the Server Manager console, click Add Roles and Features.

2. On the Before You Begin page of the Add Roles and Features wizard, click Next.

3. On the Installation Type page, click Role-Based or Feature-Based Installation and then click Next.

4. On the Select Destination Server page, ensure that the server that you want to host the Web Application Proxy server role is selected. Figure 5-57 shows the server SYD-WEBAP selected. Click Next.

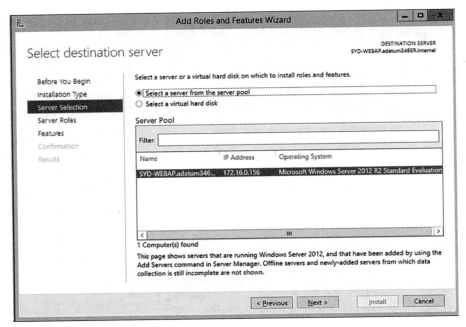

FIGURE 5-57 Select server from pool

5. On the Server Roles page, ensure that Remote Access is selected as shown in Figure 5-58 and then click Next.

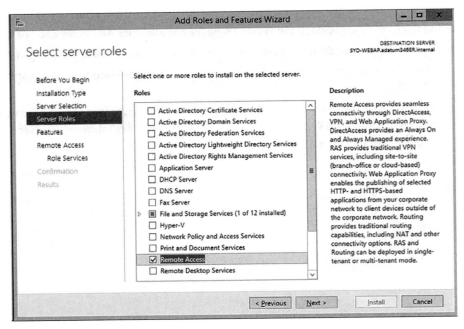

FIGURE 5-58 Remote Access

6. On the Features page, click Next.

7. On the Remote Access page, click Next.

8. On the Role Services page, select Web Application Proxy as shown in Figure 5-59, and then click Next.

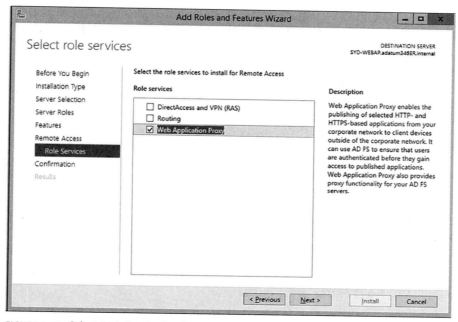

FIGURE 5-59 Select Web Application Proxy

9. On the Confirm Installation Selections page, shown in Figure 5-60, click Install.

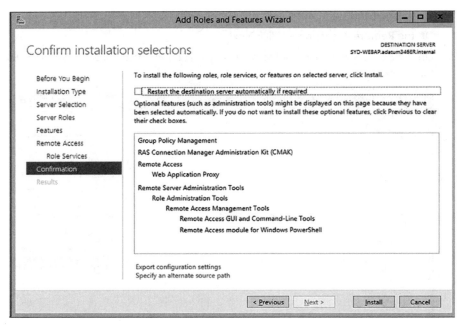

FIGURE 5-60 Confirmation Page

> **MORE INFO AD FS PROXY DEPLOYMENT**
>
> You can learn more about configuring the web application proxy at: *http://blogs.technet.com/b/rmilne/archive/2014/04/28/how-to-install-adfs-2012-r2-for-office-365_1320_part-2.aspx.*

Configuring AD FS Web Application Proxy

Once you install the Web Application Proxy role, you can configure it by performing the following steps:

1. Click the Remote Access node of the Server Manager console and click More next to Configuration Required For Web Application Proxy as shown in Figure 5-61.

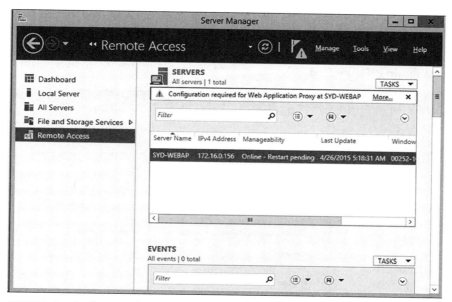

FIGURE 5-61 Configure Web Application Proxy

2. On the All Servers Task Details and Notifications page, shown in Figure 5-62, click Open the Web Application Proxy Wizard.

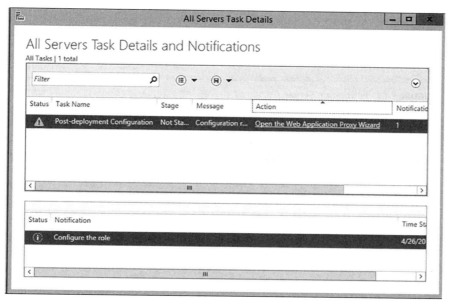

FIGURE 5-62 All Servers Task Details

3. On the Welcome page of the Web Application Proxy Configuration Wizard, click Next.

4. On the Federation Server page, enter the name of the AD FS Federation Service and provide the credentials of an account with local Administrator rights on those servers as shown in Figure 5-63.

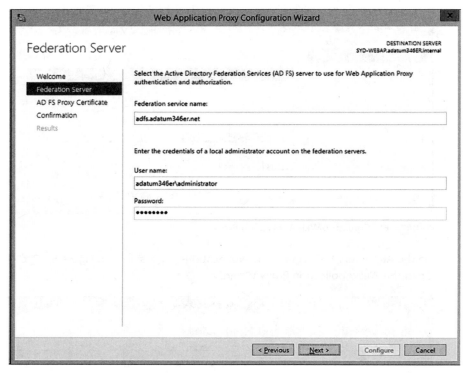

FIGURE 5-63 Federation Server

5. On the AD FS Proxy Certificate page, select the AD FS Service Communications Certificate, which you have already installed in the Personal Certificate store of the Web Application Proxy server's computer account as shown in Figure 5-64 and click Next.

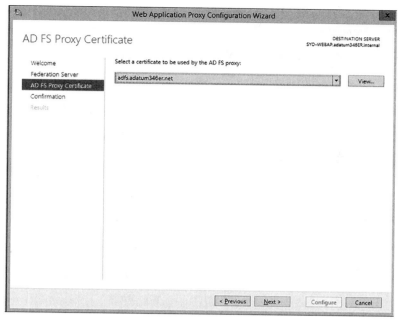

FIGURE 5-64 AD FS Proxy Certificate

6. On the Confirmation page, shown in Figure 5-65, review the information and then click Configure.

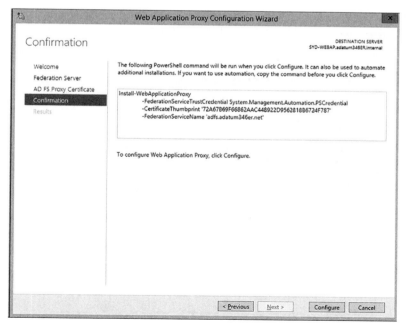

FIGURE 5-65 Confirmation

7. On the Results page, verify that the Web Application Proxy was configured successfully as shown in Figure 5-66.

FIGURE 5-66 Confirmation

To confirm that the Web Application Proxy server is functioning correctly, open the Remote Access Management console and then select the Operations Status node as shown in Figure 5-67.

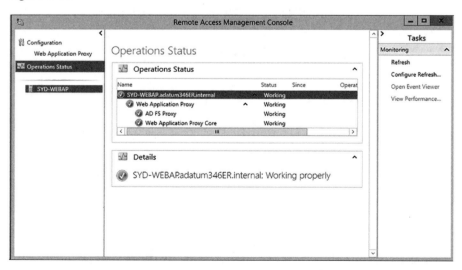

FIGURE 5-67 Verify AD FS proxy operation

Setting custom proxy forms login page

You can customize the proxy form login so that it better represents the need of your organization. You do this by using a specific set of Windows PowerShell commands.

To set the company name, use the Set-AdfsGlobalWebContent cmdlet with the CompanyName parameter. For example, to set the company name to "Adatum Hovercraft" use the following PowerShell command:

```
Set-AdfsGlobalWebContent -CompanyName "Adatum Hovercraft"
```

You can change the company logo displayed on the sign-in page with an image file in PNG format that has a resolution of 260 pixels by 35 and which is no greater than 10 KB in size using the Set-AdfsWebTheme cmdlet with the Logo parameter. For example, to set the company logo to a file named c:\logos\logo.png, issue the following command:

```
Set-AdfsWebTheme -TargetName default -Logo @{path="c:\logos\logo.png"}
```

To change the large illustrative graphic on the left, you use the Set-AdfsWebTheme cmdlet with the –Illustration parameter. The file for the illustration should be 1420 pixels by 1080 pixels in PNG format and should be no larger than 200 KB. For example, to set the illustration to the file illustration.png in the folder c:\illustrations, issue the following command:

```
Set-AdfsWebTheme -Targetname default -Illustration @{Path="c:\illustrations\
illustration.png}
```

You can add a sign-in page description using the Set-AdfsGlobalWebContent cmdlet with the SignInPageDescriptionText parameter. For example, to add the text "Welcome to the Adatum single sign on page", issue the command:

```
Set-AdfsGlobalWebContent -SignInPageDescriptionText "Welcome to the Adatum single signon
page"
```

You can use the HelpDeskLink parameter with the Set-AdfsGlobalWebContent cmdlet to configure a help desk link, the HomeLink parameter to specify a home link, and the PrivacyLink parameter to add a privacy link.

Password synchronization as fallback

In the event that your organization's on-premises single sign on servers become unavailable, it's possible to temporarily switch to password synchronization until the issue with the single-sign on infrastructure is resolved. You can do this using the Azure AD Connect tool covered in more detail in "Chapter 4, Implement and manage identities by usin Azure AD connect" and use it as a form of backup technology for AD FS SSO. Important to note that this process is not instantaneous and may take several hours to complete.

> **MORE INFO SWITCHING FROM SSO TO PASSWORD SYNC**
>
> You can learn more about switching from SSO to Password Sync at: *https://social.technet.microsoft.com/wiki/contents/articles/17857.dirsync-how-to-switch-from-single-sign-on-to-password-sync.aspx.*

Thought experiment

In this thought experiment, demonstrate your skills and knowledge of the topics covered in this chapter. You can find answers to this through experiment in the next section.

You are the systems administrator at Margie's Travel. You want to configure multi-factor authentication for your AD FS 4.0 single sign-on solution for Office 365. You also want to ensure that the password used with the AD FS service account password is changed on a regular basis, but you want to minimize the amount of direct intervention needed to perform this task. Rather than have the AD FS configuration wizard configure the Service Principal Name (SPN), you want to perform this task manually. You are also interested in changing the default proxy forms logon page for your organization's AD FS deployment used to support Office 365. You want to change the logo to a file named c:\images\newlogo.png, you want to change the illustration to a file named c:\images\newillustration.png and you want to change the company name to Tailspin Toys.

With this information in mind, answer the following questions:

1. What do you need to download and install to support multi-factor authentication for Office 365 single sign-on?
2. What secondary authentication methods are supported for Office 365 multi-factor authentication when single sign-on is configured using AD FS?
3. What service account option should you use?
4. Which utility can you use to set the SPN for the AD FS service account manually?
5. What Windows PowerShell command should you use to change the logo?
6. What Windows PowerShell command should you use to change the illustration?
7. What Windows PowerShell command should you use to change the company name?

Thought experiment answers

This section contains the solution to the thought experiment. Each letter explains why the answer choice is correct or incorrect.

1. You can configure multi-factor authentication for Office 365 single sign-on by downloading and installing the Azure Multi-Factor Authentication Server.

2. You can configure the following secondary authentication methods Phone call, text message, mobile app, and OAUTH token

3. You should configure a group managed service account to ensure that passwords are managed by Active Directory and don't have to be changed manually.

4. You use the setspn.exe utility to configure the SPN for the AD FS service account manually.

5. You should use the command Set-AdfsWebTheme -TargetName default -Logo @ {path="c:\images\logo.png"}

6. You should use the command Set-AdfsWebTheme -TargetName default -Illustration @ {path="c:\Contoso\illustration.png"}

7. You should use the command: Set-AdfsGlobalWebContent –CompanyName "Contoso Corp"

Chapter summary

- An AD FS farm consists of one or more servers running AD FS.

- The Service Communications Certificate's subject name and Subject Alternative Name must include the federation service name.

- The Service Communications Certificate's Subject Alternative Name must contain the value enterpriseregistration and the UPN suffix of the organization.

- The Service Communications Certificate cannot be a wildcard certificate.

- The Service Communications Certificate must be stored in the local computer account's Personal certificate store.

- The Service Communications Certificate must be issued by a trusted third party CA.

- The name of the AD FS service must be resolvable through public DNS to the IP address of the Web Application Proxy server.

- Multi-Factor authentication can be configured for AD FS by installing the Azure Multi-Factor Authentication Server and connecting it to the on-premises AD FS farm.

- You can filter access to Office 365 by configuring claim rules once you have established federation.

- AD FS 3.0 and AD FS 4.0 can use Group Managed Service Accounts.

- If configuring a service account manually, ensure that the password is set not to expire and that the account has been granted the Log on As A Service and the Log On As A Batch Job rights.

- The AD FS configuration wizard sets the SPN for the service account automatically during setup. You can do this manually with the Setspn.exe command.

- When adding additional servers, you will need to import the Service Communications Certificate, including the private key, to the Private certificate store of each additional potential AD FS server in the farm.

- You must use the same Service Account when adding potential AD FS servers to a farm. This account must be granted the Log On As A Service and the Log on As A Batch Job rights on each potential AD FS server.

- To specify the AD FS server prior to converting a standard Office 365 domain to a federated domain, use the Set-MsolADFSContext cmdlet.

- To convert a standard Office 365 domain to a federated Office 365 domain, use the Convert-MsolDomainToFederated cmdlet.

- The computer that hosts the web application proxy server role on the perimeter network must be able to resolve the IP address of the AD FS service to an AD FS server on the internal network.

- The AD FS Service Communications Certificate must be installed in the computer account's Personal certificate store.

- The Web Application Proxy role service is part of the Remote Access role.

- Configuring the Web Application Proxy role service requires that you specify the federation service name and enter the credentials of an account that has local administrator privileges on the AD FS servers.

Monitor and troubleshoot Office 365 availability and usage

Office 365 provides a large number of reports that allow organizations to determine exactly how subscribed users are using the service. There is also a multitude of ways that you can monitor Office 365; from using the built in reporting functionality to deploying a special Office 365 management pack for System Center Operations Manager. Finally, Microsoft provides a number of different tools that you can use to troubleshoot Office 365 should it, or specific Office 365 functionality, become unavailable.

Skills in this chapter:

- Skill 6.1: Analyze reports
- Skill 6.2: Monitor service health
- Skill 6.3: Isolate service interruption

Skill 6.1: Analyze reports

This skill deals with several of the reports that are available through the Office 365 admin center. To master this skill, you'll need to understand the types of reports that are available and the information these reports display.

> **This section covers the following topics:**
> - Mail reports
> - Usage reports
> - Auditing reports
> - Protection reports

Office 365 reports

Office 365 offers a large number of reports, shown in Figure 6-1, that tenant administrators can use to learn how an organization consumes Office 365 services. It's possible to view these reports either through the web console, or to export the data from these reports into a format that can be displayed in Microsoft Excel. Office 365 also supports the creation of custom reports through the Office 365 web services. A user must be a global administrator in Office 365 to view reports at the Office 365 level.

FIGURE 6-1 List of available reports

MORE INFO **OFFICE 365 REPORTS**

You can learn more about Office 365 reports at: *https://support.office.com/en-us/article/ View-and-download-reports-about-service-usage-in-Office-365-30e5558f-d3c0-4a3b-a0d5-58fc7750c0ad?omkt=en-us&ui=en-US&rs=en-US&ad=US.*

Activations

The Office Activation report provides data on the users who have activated their Office 365 subscription on one or more devices. You can use it to determine activations for Office 365 ProPlus, Project, and Visio Pro for Office 365. You can also view activation information including whether the product was activated on a computer running Windows, macOS, or devices running the iOS or Android mobile operating systems. This report is displayed in Figure 6-2.

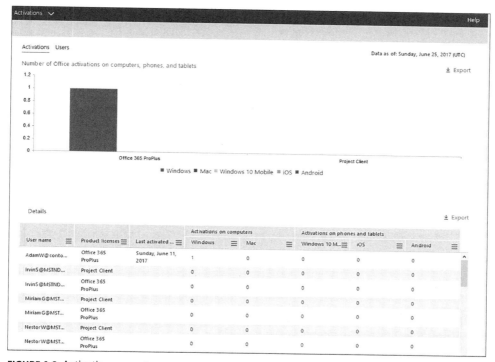

FIGURE 6-2 Activations reports

> **MORE INFO** **ACTIVATIONS REPORT**
>
> You can learn more about the Activations report at: *https://support.office.com/client/ Office-activations-87c24ae2-82e0-4d1e-be01-c3bcc3f18c60.*

Active users

The Active Users report, shown in Figure 6-3, provides information on the number of product licenses that are being used across your organization. It also provides you with information about the products licensed by specific users. You can use this report to determine which products are not fully being used.

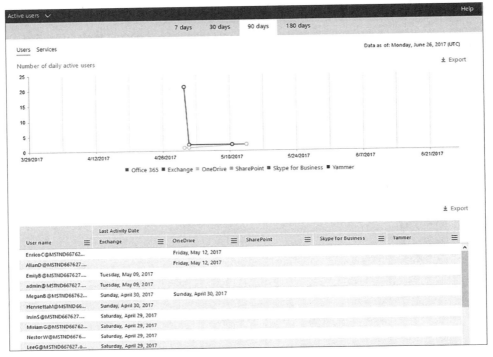

FIGURE 6-3 Active Users report

> **MORE INFO ACTIVE USERS REPORT**
>
> You can learn more about the Active Users report at: *https://support.office.com/client/ Active-Users-fc1cf1d0-cd84-43fd-adb7-a4c4dfa8112d.*

Office 365 groups activity

The Office 365 groups report allows you to view information about Office 365 groups. This includes the total number of groups, the number of active groups, and the storage used by group mailboxes, as shown in Figure 6-4. Activity information includes the number of messages received, the item count, the size of items, and whether or not those items are public.

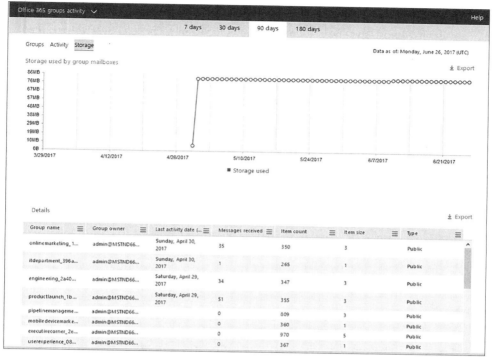

FIGURE 6-4 Office 365 Groups Activity Report

> **MORE INFO** **OFFICE 365 GROUPS ACTIVITY REPORT**
>
> You can learn more about the Office 365 Groups Activity Report at: *https://support.office.com/client/Office-365-groups-a27f1a99-3557-4f85-9560-a28e3d822a40.*

Exchange reports

Exchange reports are available through the Office 365 Admin Center and provide information about Exchange Online messaging traffic and activity. A user must be either an Office 365 global administrator, or an Exchange administrator to view Exchange reports. There available Exchange reports are as follows:

- Email activity
- Mailbox usage
- Email app usage

Email Activity

The Email Activity report, shown in Figure 6-5, shows the number of send, receive, and read actions across the organization, with a per user breakdown. You can use this report to get high level information about email traffic at your organization, including the last activity date, the number of send actions, receive actions, and read actions. You can use this report to view email activity over the last 7 days, 30 days, 90 days and 180 days.

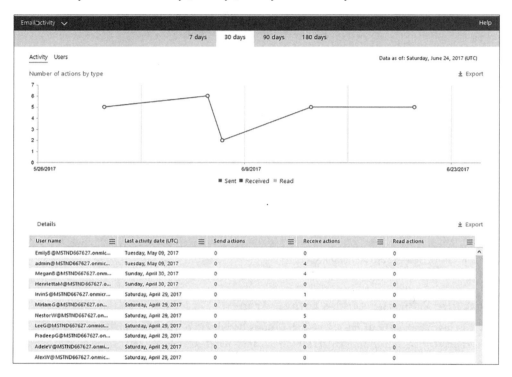

FIGURE 6-5 Email Activity report

> **MORE INFO EMAIL ACTIVITY REPORT**
>
> You can learn more about the email activity report at: *https://support.office.com/client/ Email-activity-1cbe2c00-ca65-4fb9-9663-1bbfa58ebe44.*

Mailbox Usage

This mailbox usage report, shown in Figure 6-6, shows the total number of mailboxes, the total number of active user mailboxes, the amount of storage used across all mailboxes, and the mailboxes by quota status (good, warning issued, send prohibited, and send/receive prohibited). You can also view the number of deleted items, the last activity date, and the number of items in each user's mailbox. The report allows you to view data from the last 7 days, 30 days, 90 days and 180 days.

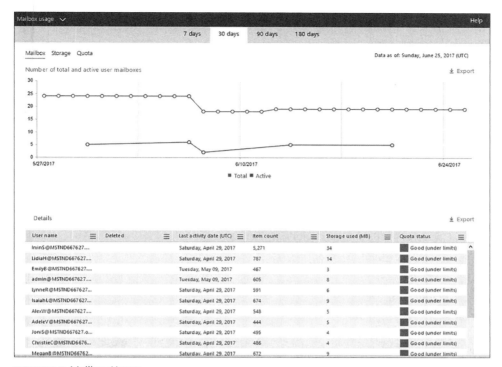

FIGURE 6-6 Mailbox Usage

> **MORE INFO MAILBOX USAGE REPORT**
>
> You can learn more about the mailbox usage report at: *https://support.office.com/client/ Mailbox-usage-beffbe01-ce2d-4614-9ae5-7898868e2729*.

Email App usage

The Email App Usage report provides information on the email app used by each user to access Exchange Online. Each app used to interact with Exchange Online is tracked, so you can determine the app usage profile of each user. This report tracks usage through Outlook on Windows, Outlook on macOS, Outlook on the web, as well as mobile clients.

> **MORE INFO EMAIL APP USAGE REPORT**
>
> You can learn more about the email app usage report at: *https://support.office.com/client/ Email-apps-usage-c2ce12a2-934f-4dd4-ba65-49b02be4703d*.

OneDrive

The OneDrive reports provide information about how OneDrive for Business is used through-
out your Office 365 organization. There are two reports, the OneDrive activity report, and
the OneDrive usage report. In these reports, the product name OneDrive and OneDrive
for Business are used interchangeably. Outside of the reports interface, the name OneDrive
denotes the consumer offering and the OneDrive for Business the cloud storage option that is
associated with Office 365.

OneDrive activity

The OneDrive activity report, also known as the OneDrive for Business Activity Report, allows
you to view the activity of all Office 365 OneDrive for Business users. This report, shown in
Figure 6-7, provides information on the following:

- Last OneDrive for Business Activity
- Files viewed or edited
- Files synced
- Files shared internally
- Files shared externally

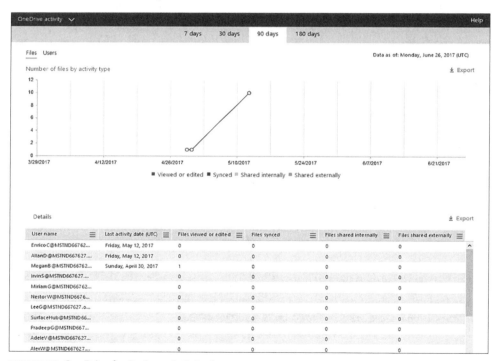

FIGURE 6-7 OneDrive for Business Activity Report

OneDrive usage

The OneDrive usage report, also known as the OneDrive for Business usage report, provides a high-level overview of how files are used in your organization's OneDrive for Business subscription. The report, shown in Figure 6-8, provides details of the following:

- **URL**   This is the file's location within OneDrive for Business
- **Owner**   Office 365 account associated with the file
- **Last activity date (UTC)**   Last date that the file was accessed
- **Files**   Number of files associated with the user
- **Active files**   Number of user's files being actively used
- **Storage used (MB)**   Storage consumed by the user's files

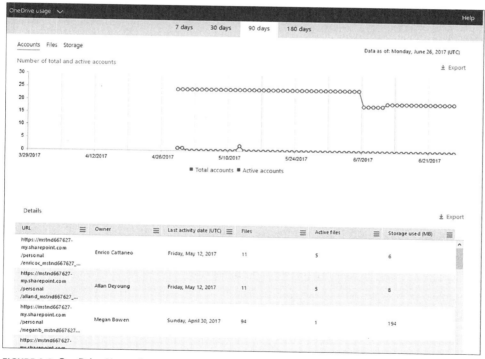

FIGURE 6-8 OneDrive Usage Report

Skype for Business

Skype for Business reports, sometimes termed Skype for Business Online reports, provide information on how an organization's Skype for Business implementation is being used by Office 365 users. These reports are visible to Office 365 global administrators and Skype for Business Administrators

Skype for Business Activity

The Skype for Business activity report provides you with information on Skype for Business activity on a per-user basis across your Office 365 organization. This includes information on the following:

- Last activity date
- Peer-to-peer
- Organized conferences
- Participated in conferences

Skype for Business Peer-To-Peer Activity

The Skype for Business Online Peer-To-Peer Activity report provides information about communication that occurs between individual Skype for Business users outside of Skype for Business conferences. This report tracks the following activity on a per-user basis:

- Last activity date
- Number of peer-to-peer Instant Messaging sessions
- Number of peer-to-peer audio conferences
- Number of peer-to-peer video conferences
- Number of peer-to-peer application sharing sessions
- Number of peer-to-peer file transfers
- Number of minutes spent in peer-to-peer audio conferences
- Number of minutes spent in peer-to-peer video conferences

MORE INFO SKYPE FOR BUSINESS PEER-TO-PEER ACTIVITY REPORT

You can learn more about the Skype for Business Peer-to-Peer report at: *https://support. office.com/client/Skype-for-Business-Online-peertopeer-activity-d3b2d569-4ee9-44b8- 92bf-d518142f0713.*

Skype for Business Conference Organizer Activity

The Skype for Business Conference Organizer Activity Report provides information about conferences initiated by your organization's Skype for Business users. This report presents the following information over a 7 day, 30 day, 90 day, and 180 day time frame by username:

- Last activity
- IM sessions organized
- Audio and Video sessions organized
- Application sharing conferences organized
- Web conferences organized
- Dial-in/out – 3rd party conferences organized
- Total audio/video minutes of conferences organized by this user
- Total number of minutes where Microsoft functioned as the dial-in audio conferencing provider
- Total number of minutes where Microsoft functioned as the dial-out audio conferencing provider

MORE INFO SKYPE FOR BUSINESS CONFERENCE ORGANIZER ACTIVITY REPORT

You can learn more about the Skype for Business Conference Organizer Activity report at: *https://support.office.com/client/Skype-for-Business-Online-conference-organized-activity- 03a255d4-0e1d-4b24-b73d-7a62fae36254.*

Skype for Business Conference Participant Activity

The Skype for Business Conference Participant Activity report provides information about Skype for Business from a participant, rather than an organizer perspective. This report includes the following information on a per-user basis:

- Last activity date
- Number of IM conferences the user participated in
- Number of audio and video conferences the user participated in
- Number of application sharing conferences that the user participated in
- Number of web conferences that the user participated in
- Number of Dial-in/out – 3rd party conferences that the user participated in using a 3rd party audio conferencing provider where Skype for Business was used for audio
- Total audio and video minutes

Skype for Business Device Usage

The Skype for Business Device Usage report, also known as the Skype for Business Client Used report, provides you with information on the specifics of clients and devices. This report provides information about Skype for Business utilization on a per user basis. You can use this report to determine which specific devices a particular user uses to access Skype for Business, with the report offering the following information:

- Last activity
- Windows based operating system
- Windows Phone based operating system
- Android mobile operating system
- iPad operating system

SharePoint

The following SharePoint reports are available through the Office 365 Admin Center to users that have the Office 365 global administrator or SharePoint administrator privileges.

SharePoint Activity

The SharePoint Activity report allows you to track how Office 365 users in your organization interact with SharePoint Online. This report provides the following information on a per-user basis:

- **Last activity date**   The last time the user interacted with SharePoint Online.
- **Files viewed or edited**   This is the number of files that the user interacted with that were hosted on the organization's SharePoint Online instance.
- **Files synced**   This is the number of files that have synchronized between the devices used by the user and SharePoint Online.
- **Files shared internally**   The number of files shared with other Office 365 users through SharePoint Online.
- **Files shared externally**   The number of files shared through Office 365 with external users.

SharePoint Site Usage

The SharePoint Site Usage report, shown in Figure 6-9, provides information on how Share-Point sites in your organization's SharePoint Online deployment, are used. This report pro-vides you with the following information:

- **Site URL** The address of the site within your SharePoint deployment
- **Site owner** Office 365 user assigned ownership of the site
- **Last Activity date** Last time activity was recorded against the site
- **Files** Number of files stored on the SharePoint online site
- **Files viewed or edited** Files that have recently been viewed or modified
- **Storage used** The amount of storage consumed by files on the site

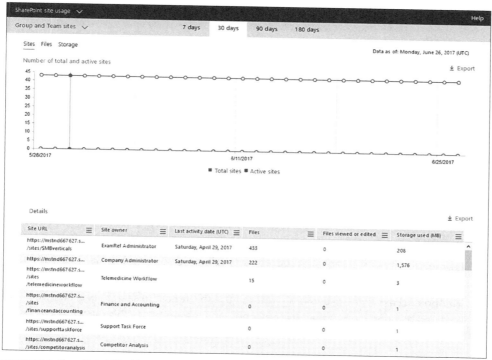

FIGURE 6-9 SharePoint Site Usage Report

Security and compliance reports

Office 365 security and compliance reports, shown in Figure 6-10, are split across four catego-ries. These reports allow you to view how security and compliance rules and technologies are being used across your Office 365 organization.

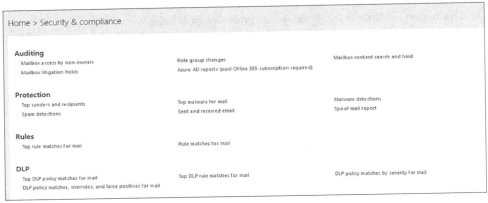

FIGURE 6-10 Security and Compliance Report Categories

Auditing reports

The following security and compliance reports are available through the Office 365 Admin Center:

- **Mailbox access by non-owners** You can use this report to search for mailboxes accessed by people other than their owners. One reason to use this report would be to check whether users with Administrative privileges have accessed certain Office 365 mailboxes.
- **Role group changes** This report allows you to view changes made to administrator role groups.
- **Mailbox content search and hold** This report provides information on all In-Place eDiscovery & Hold operations performed across the Office 365 subscription.

- **Mailbox litigation holds**   This report shows all mailboxes that are configured for litigation hold.
- **Azure AD reports**   This option allows you to view Azure Active Directory reports. It requires a paid Azure Active Directory subscription.

Protection reports

The following protection reports are available through the Office 365 Admin Center:

- **Top senders and recipients**   This report allows you to view the top mail senders, the top mail recipients, the top spam recipients, and the top malware recipients across the Office 365 subscription.
- **Top malware for mail**   This report shows the amount of malware received through e-mail for the reporting period.
- **Malware detections**   This report shows the amount of malware sent and received through the Office 365 subscription for the reporting period.
- **Spam detections**   This report shows the amount of spam on the basis of the content being filtered or the original sending host being blocked.
- **Sent and received mail**   This report shows the amount of sent and received mail categorized by good mail, malware, spam, and messages dealt with by rules.

Rules reports

The following rules reports are available through the Office 365 Admin Center:

- **Top rule matches for mail**   This report allows you to view the number of messages based on sent and received transport rule matches.
- **Rule matches for mail**   This report shows all rule matches for received and sent email.

Data Loss Prevention reports

The following Data Loss Prevention (DLP) reports are available through the Office 365 Admin Center:

- **Top DLP policy matches for mail**   Allows you to view the top DLP policy matches for sent and received email.
- **Top DLP rule matches for mail**   Allows you to view the top DLP rule matches for sent and received email.
- **DLP policy matches by severity for mail**   Allows you to track DLP policy matches by severity.
- **DLP policy matches, overrides, and false positives for mail**   Allows you to view DLP matches, overrides, and false positives for incoming and outgoing messages.

Skill 6.2: Monitor service health

This skill deals with determining whether a specific element of Office 365 is not functioning properly or is undergoing maintenance. To master this skill you'll need to understand what you can learn by accessing the service health dashboard, what you can learn using the Office 365 management pack for System Center Operations Manager, as well as what you can learn about the messaging environment using Windows PowerShell.

> **This section covers the following topics:**
> - Service health dashboard
> - RSS feed
> - Office 365 Management Pack
> - Windows PowerShell cmdlets

Service Health dashboard

The Service Health dashboard allows you to view the health of all of the services related to your organization's Office 365 subscription. For example, the screenshot of the Service Health dashboard shown in Figure 6-11 shows that the Exchange and Power BI services have advisories. It also shows that other services are reported as being healthy.

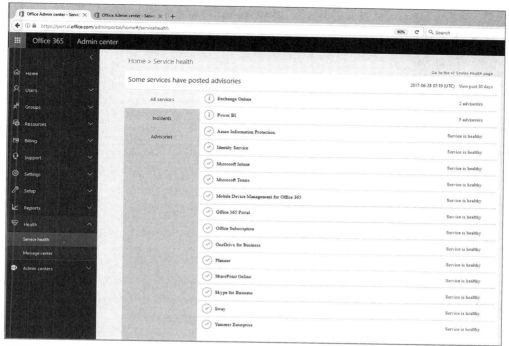

FIGURE 6-11 Service Health dashboard

History

By clicking History, you can view the status history of services over the past 30 days as shown in Figure 6-12. This may allow you to diagnose issues that may have occurred previously that you were not aware of, such as if you needed to provide an explanation to a user as to why they were unable to access specific functionality over the weekend.

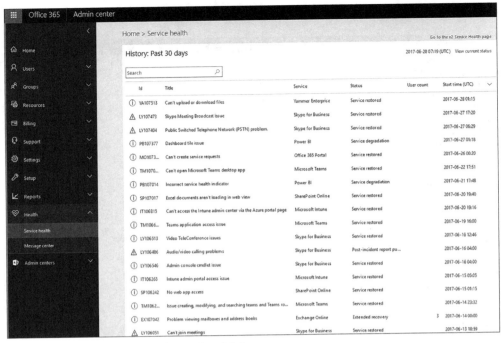

FIGURE 6-12 Service health over the previous 30 days

Planned Maintenance

Office 365 provides administrators with information about upcoming maintenance events through planned maintenance notifications. You can view planned maintenance events by navigating to the message center and setting the view to Plan For Change, as shown in Figure 6-13.

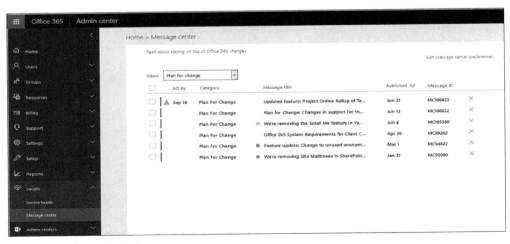

FIGURE 6-13 Planned maintenance

RSS feed

The exam objectives mention using the RSS feed to obtain information about Office 365 service health. According to the following blog post *https://blogs.technet.microsoft.com/undocumentedfeatures/2015/10/12/subscribe-to-the-office-365-service-health-dashboard-rss-feed-in-outlook/* the RSS feed is deprecated and, depending on your Office 365 region, may no longer be available.

Office 365 Management Pack

The Office 365 Management Pack for System Center Operations Manager allows you to monitor the status of one or more Office 365 subscriptions from your on-premises Operations Manager deployment. System Center Operations Manager is Microsoft's monitoring solution. Management Packs are add-on components that allow you to monitor specific products. Management Packs are available not only for Office 365, but for almost all Microsoft products like Exchange Server and SQL Server, as well as for a large number of third party products.

Installing the Office 365 Management Pack

To install the Office 365 Management Pack for System Center Operations Manager, perform the following steps:

1. Download the Office 365 Management Pack from *https://www.microsoft.com/en-us/download/details.aspx?id=43708* to the Desktop of the Operations Manager server.

2. Double click on the System Center Management Pack for Office 365 MSI installer file.

3. On the License Agreement page, click I Accept and then click Next.

4. On the Select Installation Folder page, shown in Figure 6-14, accept the default location and then click Next, click Install, and click Close.

FIGURE 6-14 Select installation folder

5. Open the Operations Manager console and then select the Administration workspace.

6. Select the Management Packs node as shown in Figure 6-15 and then click Import Management Packs from the Tasks pane.

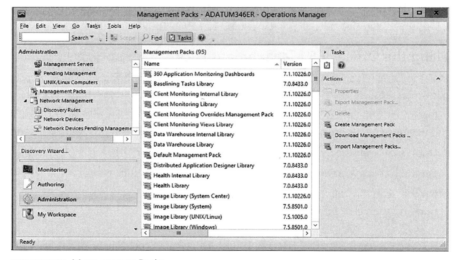

FIGURE 6-15 Management Packs

7. On the Import Management Packs dialog box, click Add and then click Add From Disk.

8. On the Online Catalog Connection Page, shown in Figure 6-16, click Yes.

FIGURE 6-16 Online Catalog Connection

9. In the Select Management Packs To Import dialog box, navigate to C:\Program Files (x86)\System Center Management Packs\System Center Management Pack for Office 365\ and select Microsoft.SystemCenter.O365.mpb as shown in Figure 6-17 and then click Open.

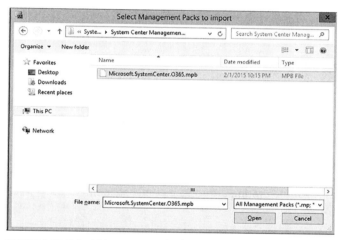

FIGURE 6-17 Select Management Packs to Import

10. On the Import Management Packs dialog box, ensure that Microsoft Office 365 is selected as shown in Figure 6-18 and then click Install. When the import completes, click Close.

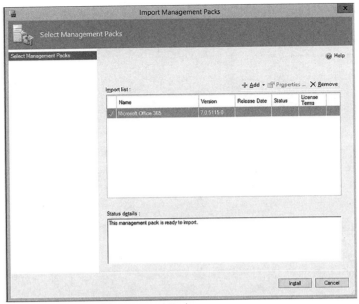

FIGURE 6-18 Import Management Packs

Configuring Office 365 for use with the management pack

Prior to configuring the Office 365 Management Pack to monitor a specific subscription, you need to create a special Office 365 user that has Global Administrator permissions to the subscription that can be used for monitoring purposes by the management pack. To do this, perform the following steps.

1. In the Office 365 Admin Center, click Users and then click Active Users.

2. On the Views drop down, select Global Admins as shown in Figure 6-19.

FIGURE 6-19 Global Admins

3. In the list of Global Admins, click the +User icon to open the Create New User Account dialog box.

4. In the Create New User Account dialog box, provide a name and password. This account will be used to allow the management pack to communicate with the Office 365 subscription, so you should choose a name that reflects that function. For example, creating an account named adatum346ERmonitor@adatum346er.onmicrosoft.com indicates that the account is used for something other than a standard user's access to Office 365.

5. Once the account is created, assign and then verify that the account has been assigned the Global Administrator role.

Configuring the Management Pack

To configure the Office 365 management pack to work with your Office 365 subscription, perform the following steps:

1. In the Administration node of the Operations Manager console click the Office 365 node as shown in Figure 6-20.

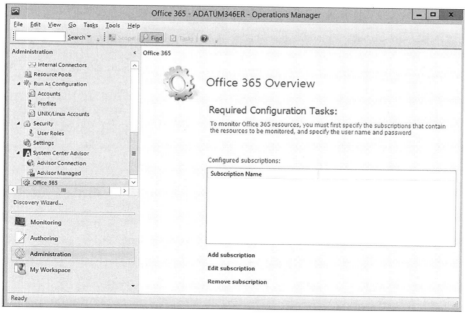

FIGURE 6-20 Office 365 node

2. On the Office 365 Overview page, click Add Subscription. This will open the Add Subscription Wizard.

3. On the Subscription Details page, specify a subscription name and the password for that account. This will be the name of the account you set up to monitor the subscription. Figure 6-21 shows this information provided for the Adatum346ER subscription.

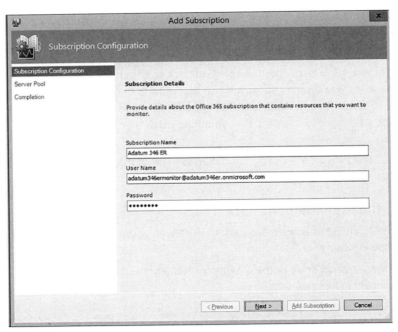

FIGURE 6-21 Subscription Configuration

4. On the Server Pool page, accept the default as shown in Figure 6-22 and click Add Subscription.

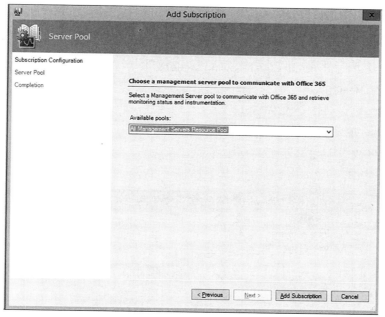

FIGURE 6-22 Server Pool

5. Verify that you get the message that the Office 365 Subscription is ready for monitoring as shown in Figure 6-23 and click Finish.

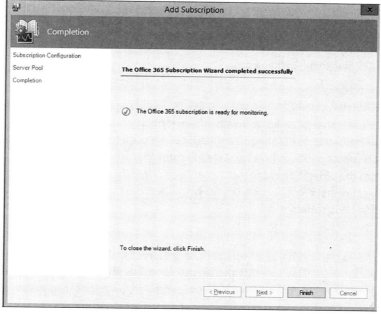

FIGURE 6-23 Wizard complete

Office 365 Monitoring Dashboard

Once you have installed the Office 365 Management Pack, you can access the Monitoring Dashboard through the Monitoring node of the Operations Manager console. This dashboard is shown in Figure 6-24 and includes the following sections:

- Subscription Health
- Service Status
- Active Incidents
- Resolved Incidents
- Message Center

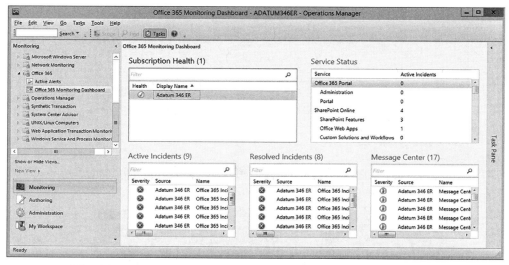

FIGURE 6-24 Office 365 Monitoring Dashboard

SUBSCRIPTION HEALTH

The Subscription Health area provides you with information of each of the monitored Office 365 subscriptions. The Office 365 Management Pack can be used to monitor the status of multiple Office 365 subscriptions. A healthy state indicates that a connection has been successfully made from the Operations Manager instance to a specific Office 365 subscription. A critical state indicates that a connection cannot be made from the Operations Manager instance to the Office 365 subscription.

SERVICE STATUS

The Service Status area displays a tree of services and features for the subscription selected in the Subscription Health area. This area lists the Service as well as any active incidents related to that service. For example, for the Adatum346ER subscription, data for the following services and features is displayed:

- Office 365 Portal

- Administration
- Portal
- SharePoint Online
  - SharePoint Features
  - Office Web Apps
  - Custom Solutions and Workflows
  - Provisioning
  - Search and Delve
  - Tenant Admin
  - Access Services
  - SP Designer
  - InfoPath Online
  - Project Online
- Lync Online
  - Audio and Video
  - Instant Messaging
  - Sign-In
  - Presence
  - All Features
  - Dial-In Conferencing
  - Federation
  - Online Meetings
  - Mobility
  - Management and Provisioning
- Identity Service
  - Administration
  - Sign-In
- Rights Management Service
  - RMS Available
- Mobile Device Management
- Office Subscription
  - Network Availability
  - Office Professional Plus Download
  - Licensing and Renewal
- Exchange Online

- Voice Mail
- E-Mail timely delivery
- Sign-in
- Yammer Enterprise
  - Yammer Components

ACTIVE INCIDENTS

The Active Incidents area displays a list of alerts for currently active Office 365 incidents for the subscription selected in the Subscription Health area. Each alert contains information about the list of affected services, features, and the status of those features. Figure 6-25 shows the properties of an alert.

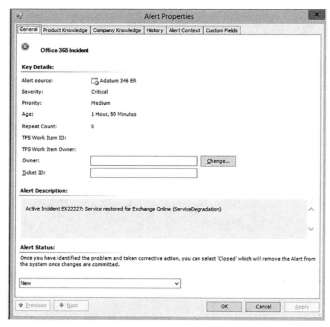

FIGURE 6-25 Alert Properties

Alerts can have one of the following states:
- Information Unavailable
- Investigating
- Service Interruption
- Service Degradation
- Restoring Service
- Extended Recovery

RESOLVED INCIDENTS

The Resolved Incidents section shows a list of resolved alerts for the currently selected subscription. Figure 6-26 shows the properties of a resolved alert.

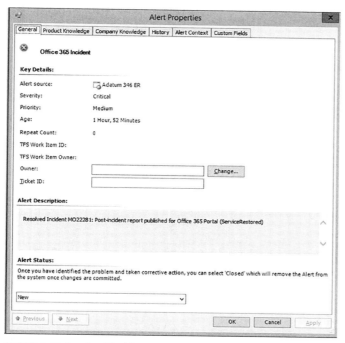

FIGURE 6-26 Resolved incident

MESSAGE CENTER

The Message Center provides a list of information messages related to the Office 365 subscription. Each alert in the Message Center will provide an external link to an article or blog post with details. Figure 6-27 shows the properties of a message from the Message Center.

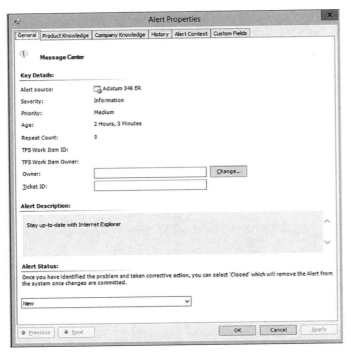

FIGURE 6-27 Message

> **MORE INFO OFFICE 365 MANAGEMENT PACK**
>
> You can learn more about the Office 365 Management Pack for System Center Operations Manager at: *http://blogs.office.com/2014/07/29/new-office-365-admin-tools/.*

Windows PowerShell cmdlets

There are a number of auditing and reporting related Windows PowerShell cmdlets that you can use with the messaging element of your organization's Office 365 subscription.

Windows PowerShell cmdlets related to message auditing include:

- **Search-AdminAuditLog**   Search the administrator audit log.
- **Write-AdminAuditLog**   Add entries to the administrator audit log.
- **Get-AdminAuditLogConfig**   View the configuration of the administrator audit log.
- **New-AdminAuditLogSearch**   Search the administrator audit log, outputting the results as e-mail to specified recipients.

- **Get-MailboxAuditBypassAssociation** View mailboxes that are configured to by-pass mailbox audit logging.
- **Set-MailboxAuditBypassAssociation** Configure one or more mailboxes so that they bypass mailbox audit logging.
- **Search-MailboxAuditLog** Examine the contents of the mailbox audit log.
- **New-MailboxAuditLogSearch** Search the mailbox audit log, outputting the results as e-mail to specified recipients.

Windows PowerShell cmdlets related to message tracking include:

- **Get-MessageTrackingReport** Provides data from a specific message tracking re-port.
- **Search-MessageTrackingReport** Allows you to locate a specific message tracking report based on search criteria.

More comprehensive coverage of Windows PowerShell cmdlets that you can use with Of-fice 365 is provided in Chapter 3, "Manage Cloud Identities."

EXAM TIP

Remember that you need to configure an account with Global Administrator privileges in Office 365 to be used for the Office 365 Management Pack for System Center Operations Manager.

Skill 6.3: Isolate service interruption

This skill deals with tools and methods that you can use to troubleshoot issues when Office 365 or your hybrid deployment isn't functioning as expected. To master this skill you'll need to understand the different tools available from Microsoft for resolving issues, including creating a service request, the Microsoft Remote Connectivity Analyzer, the Microsoft Con-nectivity Analyzer Tool, the Transport Reliability IP Probe, and the Hybrid Free Busy Trouble-shooter.

> **This section covers the following topics:**
> - Microsoft Remote Connectivity Analyzer
> - Microsoft Connectivity Analyzer Tool
> - Transport Reliability IP Probe
> - Hybrid free/busy troubleshooter

Microsoft Remote Connectivity Analyzer

The Microsoft Remote Connectivity Analyzer is a web application that you can access at: *https://testconnectivity.microsoft.com/*. The Microsoft Remote Connectivity Analyzer allows you to perform remote tests that run from Microsoft's servers on the Internet. You can use the Microsoft Remote Connectivity Analyzer to diagnose common connectivity problems for Office 365, on-premises Exchange, Lync / OCS Server, the Outlook client, and Internet Email.

The Microsoft Remote Connectivity Analyzer supports the following tests for an on-premises Exchange deployment, as long as that deployment is running Exchange 2007 or later as shown in Figure 6-28:

- Microsoft Exchange ActiveSync Connectivity Tests
  - **Exchange ActiveSync**   Checks that clients on the internet can connect to an on-premises Exchange deployment using ActiveSync.
  - **Exchange ActiveSync Autodiscover**   Checks that clients on the Internet can be automatically configured with an on-premises Exchange deployment's settings.
- Microsoft Exchange Web Services Connectivity Tests
  - **Synchronization, Notification, Availability, and Automatic Replies**   Checks the functionality of many on-premises Exchange Web Services tasks.
  - **Service Account Access (Developers)**   Checks that a specified service account is able to access a nominated on-premises mailbox and to perform operations such as the creation and deletion of mailbox items. Also checks Exchange impersonation functionality.
- Microsoft Office Outlook Connectivity Tests
  - **Outlook Connectivity**   Checks that an Outlook client on the Internet is able to connect to the on-premises Exchange deployment.
  - **Outlook Autodiscover**   Checks that an Outlook client on the Internet can be configured with on-premises Exchange settings through Autodiscover.
- Internet E-mail Tests
  - **Inbound SMTP E-Mail**   Checks that inbound SMTP e-mail can be successfully sent to the on-premises Exchange deployment.
  - **Outbound SMTP Email**   Checks outbound SMTP configuration to ensure that Reverse DNS, Sender ID, and RBL (Realtime Blackhole List) checks are passed.
  - **POP Email**   Checks that a client can access an on-premises Exchange mailbox using the POP3 protocol.
  - **IMAP Email**   Checks that a client can access an on-premises Exchange mailbox using the IMAP4 protocol.

FIGURE 6-28 Microsoft Remote Connectivity Analyzer

Use this tool if you suspect that the on-premises component of a hybrid deployment is causing problems.

If you suspect that there is a problem with the messaging elements of Office 365, you can use the Office 365 tab of the Microsoft Remote Connectivity Analyzer to test Office functionality. These tests allow you to check basic Office 365 messaging functionality, including allowing you to assess whether or not the DNS configuration for Office 365 messaging elements is configured correctly. The following tests are available for an Office 365 deployment as shown in Figure 6-29:

- Office 365 General Tests

  - **Office 365 Exchange Domain Name Server (DNS) Connectivity Test** Checks the external domain name settings, including checking whether there are issues for mail delivery and any client connectivity issues related to DNS.

  - **Office 365 Lync Domain Name Server (DNS) Connectivity Test** Checks the external domain name settings related to Lync for a custom Office 365 domain user.

  - **Office 365 Single Sign-On Test** This test allows you to verify that it is possible to sign on to Office 365 using on-premises credentials. This test also performs basic validation of the Active Directory Federation Services configuration.

- Microsoft Exchange ActiveSync Connectivity Tests

  - **Exchange ActiveSync** This test checks whether a mobile device can connect to Office 365 messaging resources using Exchange ActiveSync.

  - **Exchange ActiveSync Autodiscover** This test checks whether a device uses Exchange ActiveSync to successfully obtain configuration settings from the Autodiscover service hosted through Office 365.

- Microsoft Exchange Web Services Connectivity Tests

  - **Synchronization, Notification, Availability, and Automatic Replies** Checks the availability and functionality of Exchange Web Services resources in the Office 365 deployment.

- **Service Account Access (Developers)**   Checks the ability for a service account to access an Office 365 mailbox, create and delete items in the mailbox, and access the mailbox through Exchange Impersonation.
- Microsoft Office Outlook Connectivity Tests
    - **Outlook Connectivity**   Checks client connectivity to Office 365 using both RPC over HTTP and MAPI over HTTP.
    - **Outlook Autodiscover**   Checks the provisioning of Office 365 settings to outlook through the Autodiscover service.
- Internet Email Tests
    - **Inbound SMTP Email**   Checks that inbound SMTP email can be sent to the Office 365 domain.
    - **Outbound SMTP Email**   Checks that the Office 365 mail domain is correctly configured for Reverse DNS, Sender ID, and RBL (Realtime Blackhole List) checks.
    - **POP Email**   Performs a POP3 client e-mail check against an Office 365 mailbox.
    - **IMAP Email**   Performs an IMAP4 client e-mail check against an Office 365 mailbox.
- Mail Flow Configuration
    - **Verify Service Delivery Test**   Checks delivery from Office 365 by sending service-generated messages to a specified IP address.
    - **Verify MX Record and Outbound Connector Test**   Verifies MX record configuration and that Office 365 is configured to enable mail delivery on the basis of this record.
- **Free/Busy Test**   Checks that an Office 365 mailbox is able to access free/busy information of an on-premises mailbox. Also checks that an on-premises mailbox is able to access the free/busy information of an Office 365 mailbox.

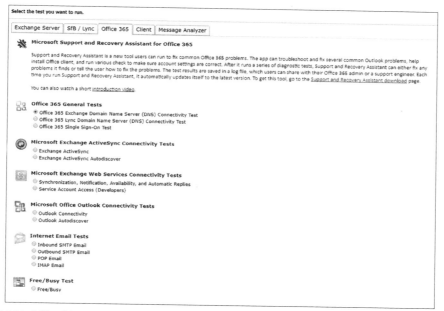

FIGURE 6-29 Office 365 tab

When you perform the test, the Microsoft Remote Connectivity Analyzer will provide details about the parts of the test that were performed successfully, any steps that failed, and possible resolution methods. Figure 6-30 shows the results of the Office 365 Exchange Domain Name Server (DNS) Connectivity test.

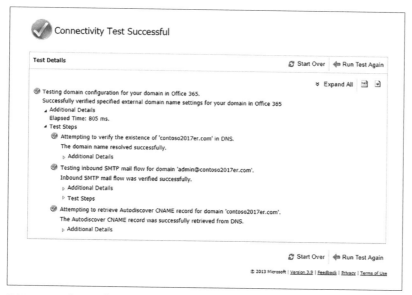

FIGURE 6-30 Successful test

MORE INFO Microsoft Remote Connectivity Analyzer

You can learn more about the Microsoft Remote Connectivity Analyzer at: *https://technet. microsoft.com/en-US/library/ff701693%28v=exchg.150%29.aspx*.

Microsoft Connectivity Analyzer

The Microsoft Connectivity Analyzer is a companion tool for the Remote Connectivity Analyzer. The main difference between these tools is that you run the Microsoft Remote Connectivity Analyzer from a website on the Internet, whereas you run the Microsoft Connectivity Analyzer from your local on-premises infrastructure. Rather than run from a web page, you download and install the tool from the Remote Connectivity Analyzer website. Note that Microsoft is replacing the Microsoft Connectivity Analyzer with the Microsoft Support and Recovery Assistant for Office 365, covered later in this chapter.

The Microsoft Connectivity Analyzer allows you to perform connectivity tests against your on-premises messaging deployment as well as against Office 365. You can use the Microsoft Connectivity Analyzer, shown in Figure 6-31, to perform the following diagnostic tests:

- **I can't log on with Office Outlook** This test checks Outlook Anywhere (RPC over HTTP) functionality.
- **I can't send or receive e-mail on my mobile device** This test checks Exchange ActiveSync functionality.
- **I can't log on to Lync on my mobile device or the Lync Windows Store app** This check verifies that DNS records have been correctly configured in your on-premises environment. It also checks the Autodiscover web service to verify that authentication and certificates are configured correctly.
- **I can't send or receive e-mail from Outlook (Office 365 Only)** This test verifies the incoming and outgoing SMTP configuration. The test will also check DNS configuration.
- **I can't view the free/busy information of another user** This test will perform a check to see if an Office 365 mailbox can access the free/busy information of an on-premises mailbox, or that an on-premises mailbox is able to access the free/busy information of an Office 365 mailbox.
- **I am experiencing other problems with Outlook (English Only)** This test checks for Outlook configuration problems.
- **I can't set up federation with Office 365, Azure, or other services that use Azure Active Directory** This test checks the prerequisites for setting up federation between an on-premises Active Directory deployment, Office 365, and Azure Active Directory.

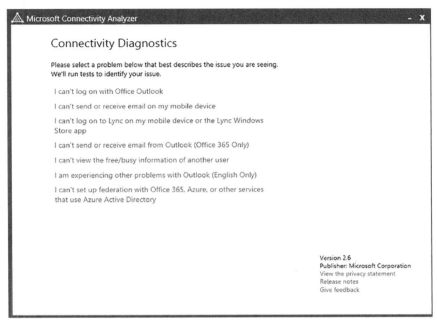

FIGURE 6-31 Connectivity Diagnostics

MORE INFO **MICROSOFT CONNECTIVITY ANALYZER**

You can learn more about Microsoft Connectivity Analyzer at: *http://blogs.technet.com/b/exchange/archive/2013/03/11/announcing-microsoft-connectivity-analyzer-mca-1-0-and-microsoft-remote-connectivity-analyzer-rca-2-1.aspx.*

Transport Reliability IP Probe

The Transport Reliability IP Probe (TRIPP) is a tool that allows you to validate the following:

- The path between a computer and a specific Lync, now termed Skype for Business, online hosting location.
- The availability of specific ports
- Routing to the Lync/Skype for Business datacenter
- Voice over IP quality
- Network speed

TRIPP performs the following tests:

- **Speed** This test will determine download and upload speed, data quality, and TCP efficiency. The test uses TCP port 443. Speeds below 1 Mbps will lead to problems with audio and video quality.

- **Rout**   This test determines route quality by measuring packet loss, latency, round trip time, and ISP peering points and test uses ICMP.

- **VoIP**   This test determines VoIP quality by assessing UDP loss and jitter. It uses UDP ports 50021 and 50022 It checks whether the round trip response time is consistent. Inconsistent round trip times may lead to choppy or jittery connections. In general, if there is more than a 5ms variance in round trip time, VoIP will be jittery. If greater than 2% packet loss is experienced, then the audio and video quality will be degraded.

- **Firewall**   This test checks the following ports:
  - TCP port 443 for Client Signaling plus AppShare
  - TCP port 5061 for Federation Signaling
  - UDP port 3478 for Media Access
  - UDP ports in range 50,000 through 59,999 for Audio/Video transport tests

Hybrid Free Busy Troubleshooter

The Hybrid Free Busy Troubleshooter is a tool that you can access at: *http://aka.ms/hybrid-freebusy*. It allows you to troubleshoot free/busy calendar issues when you have Office 365 deployed in a hybrid configuration with an on premises Exchange deployment. The Hybrid Free Busy Troubleshooter tool is designed to be used with Office 365 Tenant Administrator privileges.

Accessing the Hybrid Free Busy Troubleshooter tool gives you the following options, shown in Figure 6-32:

- My Cloud user cannot see Free/busy for an on-premises user
- My On-premises user cannot see Free/busy for a cloud user
- I want to see some common tools for troubleshooting Free/busy issues
- I want to better understand how Hybrid Free/Busy is supposed to work

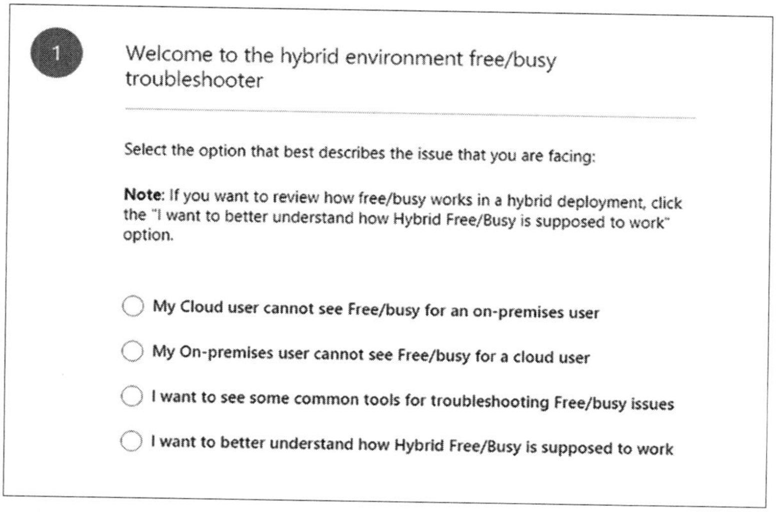

FIGURE 6-32 Hybrid Free/Busy Troubleshooter

You can use the Hybrid Free Busy Troubleshooter tool to troubleshoot free and busy issues for on-premises deployments of Exchange when your on-premises deployment uses Exchange Server 2010, Exchange Server 2013, or Exchange Server 2016.

> **MORE INFO** **HYBRID FREE/BUSY TROUBLESHOOTER**
>
> You can learn more about the Hybrid Free Busy Troubleshooter at: *https://support.microsoft.com/en-us/help/10092/troubleshooting-free-busy-issues-in-exchange-hybrid-environment*.

Support and Recovery Assistant for Office 365

The Support and Eecovery Assistant for Office 365 is a new tool available from Microsoft that is designed to allow users to troubleshoot and resolve problems related to Office 365 applications and services. Non-privileged users are able to use the Support and Recovery Assistant for Office 365, shown in Figure 6-33, to diagnose issues with Office 365 app functionality such as account configuration, connectivity issues, and crashes. You can use the Support and Recovery Assistant for Office 365 to resolve problems with Office Setup, Outlook on Windows, Outlook for Mac, mobile devices, Outlook on the web, Dynamics 365 and OneDrive for Business.

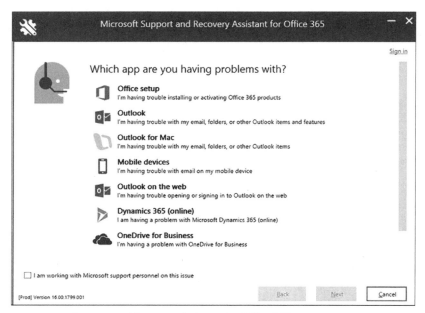

FIGURE 6-33 Support and Recovery Assistant for Office 365

The Support and Recovery Assistant for Office 365 does this by performing the following tests:

- Confirms user license
- Verifies that Office 365 servers can be contacted
- Validates user credentials
- Determines whether the client is missing any software updates
- Verifies appropriate authentication methods are being used
- Validates network functionality
- Checks protocols

Depending on the problems that the Support and Recovery Assistant may be able to resolve the problem automatically, or it may provide links to documentation that allow the user to resolve the problem themselves.

MORE INFO **SUPPORT AND RECOVERY ASSISTANCE FOR OFFICE 365**

You can learn more about the Support and Recovery Assistant for Office 365:
https://diagnostics.outlook.com/#/?env=ExRCA

EXAM TIP

Remember which tools you can use to diagnose specific problems.

Thought experiment

In this thought experiment, apply what you've learned about this objective. You can find the answers to these questions in the "Answers" section at the end of the chapter.

Contoso has recently started using Skype for Business as part of its Office 365 deployment, replacing a third party product that had similar functionality. As part of assessing the success of the adoption, management wants data on how the Skype for Business functionality available through Office 365 is being used.

You are also investigating the Windows PowerShell auditing functionality that is available for use with your organization's Office 365 messaging deployment. You are interested in configuring a bypass of audit logging for certain Office 365 mailboxes. You are also interested in performing regular searches of the admin audit log for suspicious activity.

With this information in mind, answer the following questions:

1. Which report would you access to find out about the number of Skype for Business conferences held by a specific user?

2. Which report would you access to determine the number of users leveraging Skype for Business for peer-to-peer communication?

3. Which Windows PowerShell cmdlet would you use to bypass audit logging on specific mailboxes?

4. Which Windows PowerShell cmdlet would you use to search the administrator audit log, sending the results to your manager?

5. Which tool should you use to diagnose the functionality of your Office 365 deployment from the Internet when it comes to the automatic configuration of Outlook clients?

Thought experiment answers

This section contains the solution to the thought experiment. Each answer explains why the answer choice is correct.

1. The Skype for Business Conference Organizer Activity report would provide information about the number of Skype for Business conferences held by a specific user.

2. You would use the Skype for Business Peer-to-Peer activity report to determine the number of users leveraging Skype for Business for peer-to-peer communication.

3. You would use the Set-MailboxAuditBypassAssociation cmdlet to configure an audit logging bypass on a specific mailbox.

4. You would use the New-AdminAuditLogSearch cmdlet to search the administrator audit log, outputting the results as e-mail to forward to your manager.

5. You should use the Microsoft Remote Connectivity Analyzer to check the functionality of your Office 365 deployment from the Internet.

Chapter summary

- Mail reports allow you to view how Office 365 mailboxes are used.

- Usage reports allow you to view information about browsers, operating systems, and license consumption.

- Skype for Business reports allow you to see how Skype for Business is being used in the organization.

- SharePoint reports allow you to see how SharePoint is being used with the Office 365 subscription.

- OneDrive for Business allows you to view the OneDrive for Business storage statistics.

- Auditing reports allow you to view information about auditing of mailboxes, and mailbox litigation holds.

- Protection reports allow you to view statistics about malware and spam.

- Rules reports allow you to view how transport rules are being used.

- Data Loss Prevention reports allow you to view how Data Loss Prevention rules and policies are being applied to message traffic.

- The Service Health Dashboard is available from the Office 365 Admin Center and allows you to determine the status of the various elements of Office 365, including fault history and planned maintenance.

- The Office 365 Management Pack for System Center Operations Manager allows you to monitor the status of multiple Office 365 subscriptions from your on-premises System Center Operations Manager deployment.

- You can use certain Windows PowerShell cmdlets to review the configuration of your Office 365 and on-premises messaging environment.

- The Microsoft Remote Connectivity Analyzer is a website that allows you to run diagnostic tests against your on-premises Exchange or Office 365 messaging deployment from a location on the Internet.

- The Microsoft Connectivity Analyzer is a downloadable tool that you can use to run diagnostic tests against your on-premises Exchange or Office 365 messaging deployment from a computer on the organizational network.

- The Transport Reliability IP Probe is a set of diagnostic tools that you can use to verify the functionality of Skype for Business (previously known as Lync).

- The Hybrid Free Busy Troubleshooter is a web based tool that allows you to resolve free/busy calendar issues between on-premises mailboxes and those hosted in Office 365.

- The Microsoft Support and Recovery Assistant for Office 365 allows end users to attempt to resolve problems with application interaction with Office 365.

Index

A

AADRM module 53
Active Directory. *See* Azure Active Directory
Active Directory Domains and Trusts console 112
Active Directory Domain Services (AD DS)
  deployment 97
Active Directory Federation Services (AD FS) 98, 110, 137–192
  claim rules 151–152
  configuration 155–166
  deploying topologies 138–139
  installing 156–166
  network requirements 150
  proxy servers 179–190
    certificates for 180–181
    configuration 184–189
    custom proxy forms login page 189
    installing required Windows roles and features 181–184
    setting up perimeter network name resolution 180
  requirements for 137–152
  server farm 152–179
    adding additional servers to 166–177
    configuration 155–156
  service accounts 153–155, 176–177
  stand-alone configuration 155–156
  using certificates with 139–149, 178–179
  using namespaces 149–150
  versions of 138
Active Directory objects
  cleaning up 99–102
Active Incidents 220
Active Users report 195–196
Add-MsolAdministrativeUnitMember cmdlet 91
Add-MsolForeignGroupToRole cmdlet 90
Add-MsolGroupMember cmdlet 86
Add-MsolRoleMember cmdlet 59, 86

Add-MsolScopedRoleMember cmdlet 91
AD FS Configuration Wizard 155, 160–165
administrative unit management cmdlets 91
administrator roles 3–5
  assigning 58
  billing administrator 55
  delegated administrator 56–57
  Exchange Online administrator 57
  global administrator 54–55
  management of, in Office 365 54–60
  password administrator 56
  service administrator 56
  SharePoint Online administrator 58
  Skype for Business administrator 57–58
  user management administrator 55
ADModify.NET 101–102, 104–105
ADSIEdit 101
AIP. *See* Azure Information Protection
alerts 220
aliases
  column xii
APIPA addresses 41–42
app passwords 77–79
attribute filtering 98
auditing reports 206–207
authentication
  multi-factor 75–79, 113, 150
  pass-through 110
Autodiscover CNAME records 31, 32
Azure
  rights management 42–53
Azure Active Directory 97
  Azure AD Connect requirements 111–112
  cloud identities in 63, 64
  cmdlets 85–91
  filtering 105–107
  forest account 120

R

S

About the author

 ORIN THOMAS is an MVP, a Microsoft Regional Director, an MCT, and has a string of Microsoft MCSE and MCITP certifications. He has written more than 3 dozen books for Microsoft Press on topics including Windows Server, Windows Client, Azure, Office 365, System Center, Exchange Server, Security, and SQL Server. He is an author at PluralSight and is completing a Doctorate of Information Technology at Charles Sturt University. You can follow him on Twitter at *http://twitter.com/orinthomas*.

Hear about it first.

Get the latest news from Microsoft Press sent to your inbox.

- New and upcoming books

- Special offers

- Free eBooks

- How-to articles

Sign up today at MicrosoftPressStore.com/Newsletters

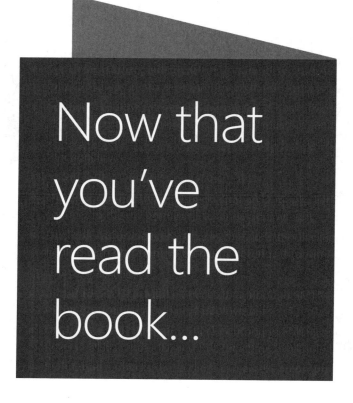

Now that you've read the book...

Tell us what you think!

Was it useful?
Did it teach you what you wanted to learn?
Was there room for improvement?

Let us know at https://aka.ms/tellpress

Your feedback goes directly to the staff at Microsoft Press,
and we read every one of your responses. Thanks in advance!